A Sabbatical Memoir
'Walking into Myself'

Sean Robertshaw

For my family
Sally, William & Lydia
& my niece Anna

© Copyright 2024 Sean Robertshaw

All rights reserved.
No part of this publication may be reproduced,
stored in a retrieval system, or transmitted, in any form or by any means,
electronic, mechanical, photocopying, recording or otherwise, without
the prior written permission of the publisher.

British Library Cataloguing in Publication Data.
A catalogue record for this book is available from the British Library.

ISBN 978 0 86071 926 7

All photography & drawings by Sean Robertshaw

List of Contents

Cover:	Figure 1. Sean and Scout, Ramsden Clough, Holmfirth
Pg 1	Introduction
	Figure 2. The Wordsworth Family Grave, St Oswald's Grasmere
Pg 2	Figure 3. Stanza Stone 'Snow' at Pule Hill Marsden
Pg 3	Beginnings
	Poem - Arrival
Pg 5	Figure 4. The Youth Hostel in Coniston, Yew Pike to the rear
Pg 7	Walking – In recent memory
Pg 8	Poem - The School Run
Pg 9	Surprise – Planning
Pg 10	Pilgrimage or Walking?
Pg 11	Poem - Mountain
Pg 12	Pruning
Pg 13	Figure 5. Clearing in a country garden near Loughrigg Tarn
Pg 15	Words
Pg 17	Longing for the Fells
	Figure 6. Route Card navigating and walking in Martindale
Pg 18	Figure 7. Ramsden Clough, Holmfirth
	Scout
Pg 20	Poem - In Retirement
	Figure 8. Scout near Wansfell Pike
Pg 21	Friendships
	Figure 9. Rev Dr Angus Stewart
Pg 22	Poem - Durham City
	Figure 10. Durham Cathedral and night
Pg 23	Figure 11. Sarah Branson leading workshop in the church community garden
Pg 24	Rain
	Figure 12. Rain flowing down the Fell sides
Pg 25	Figure 13. Flowing water: the beck falling through Ashness Bridge near Keswick
Pg 26	Company
	Figure 14. Catkins through winter snow
Pg 28	Poem - Walking
Pg 31	And my feet…
Pg 32	Figure 15. View from Orrest Head
Pg 34	Celebration
Pg 35	Topping Out
	Figure 16. Blencathra from Mungrisdale Common

Pg 36	Crossing Out
Pg 38	Poem -The Graduation
Pg 39	Back in the Lakes – Wasdale
	Figure 17. The Science Centre (Armadillo) Glasgow
Pg 40	A Visitor
Pg 41	Figure 18. View through the cloud on Scafell
Pg 42	Poem - Surprise Sun
Pg 43	Figure 19. View over Slight Side
	Yorkshire
	Figure 20. The Great Yorkshire Show
Pg 45	Another brief encounter with a stranger
	Figure 21. Exercise Arduous Serpent, Catterick, North Yorkshire
Pg 47	Poem - Moments
Pg 48	Beauty
Pg 49	Figure 22. Cotton Grass near Silver Howe
	Poem - Ground
Pg 50	Figure 23. Early Purple Orchid
Pg 51	Mountaineer
Pg 53	Poem - Raven
Pg 54	Figure 24. View from Fleetwith Pike
Pg 55	Fluid Movement
Pg 57	Figure 25. Nigel Hinchliffe Esq.
Pg 58	Figure 26. Will, Anna and Sean above Derwent Water
Pg 59	Troutbeck Revisited
Pg 60	Return
Pg 63	Poem - Wind
Pg 64	Bad News
Pg 65	Poem - Rain
	Dogs
Pg 66	Taigh Mor
Pg 69	Poem - North
	Adam
Pg 71	Figure 27. The stone cross below Great End
Pg 75	Figure 28. Sean and Simon on the Greenburn Round
Pg 76	Discovery
Pg 79	Figure 29. Latte and Cake Ambleside
Pg 80	Afterthought - Cornwall Sept 2022
Pg 81	Figure 30. Our Family
Pg 82	Thanks.
Pg 83	Drawing "Under Skiddaw"

"Sean, when you are crossing the mountains walk into yourself"
Ivy George 2022

Introduction

Every seven years Anglican clergy are invited to apply for a sabbatical. Sabbatical derives from the Hebrew *Sabat* (i.e. Sabbath). The Greek is *sabbatikos*. It is a rest or break from work. The idea of sabbatical comes from the practice of *shmita*. According to Leviticus chapter 25 the Jews in the land of Israel must take a year-long break from working their fields every seven years. In these days sabbatical has come to be understood as a break from work. Even now its meaning is not that far from its origin.

The plan for the sabbatical was to spend three months walking in the Lake District, a national park in the British Isles. My aim was to walk into myself, I came to understand this as meaning being aware of oneself, one's consciousness and motives. Herein I hope to convey some of the occurrences that have shaped me, some of the milestones I have experienced as I have journeyed, to present an insight into my own motivations, through reflective thinking, and through sharing this odyssey.

Like much of my life this writing is complex. Why am I walking? I do not really know. I think because I have always found it difficult to be still. I fidget, my mind is constantly processing. I am infrequently at rest. Why am I walking? Is it because for much of my life I have been frightened and I have been running away? '*When I was a child… but now I have put childish things behind me.*' [1 Corinthians 13:11]. Perhaps not all of them! Or could it be that I just enjoy walking? Physical activity in some way feeds me, my mind, my body, and my soul.

Another passion of mine is poetry. I had high and mighty notions of writing about and in the style of Wordsworth, Coleridge, and Robert Southey all of whom lived and worked for many years of their lives in the Lake District. They are all remembered and commemorated in Poets' Corner, Westminster Abbey. The actual work of walking drifted me away from that idea. I did not have time enough to expend in their presence; rather I wandered in their landscape. Their memory, however, remained an inspiration for writing my own poems.

Figure 2. The Wordsworth Family Grave, St Oswald's Grasmere

The sabbatical itself became a reflective and creative space which was generated by the act of walking. What was once envisioned as a pilgrimage became a walk, but more about that later.

There is little structure in this book. It is not a chronological narrative, rather we will cross various landscapes together, some come from my past that have been important way markers for me, some from the time of sabbatical. I try to use the landscape as an entrance way into a reflection. Although this memoir was written in 2022/23, I dip in and out of times in my life and the previous 25 years of parish ministry and chaplaincy. I have tried to write poetry since I was a child, so the odd attempt at a poem also appears in the script. It is my own indulgence. My overarching plan was to walk with the goal of collecting (aka bagging) the Wainwright peaks and fells which adorn the Lake District, one of the most beautiful places I have known since my childhood.

It was difficult leaving my parish and at first I seemed rooted, unable to go. On the 16th of May 2022 I found myself stranded on the top of Pule Hill in Marsden, West Yorkshire looking at a poetical collaboration between Simon Armitage the Poet Laureate and the Ilkley Literature Festival. I read the word Snow which had been cut into the quarry stones. 'Snow' is one of six poems written by Simon which appear on the Stanza Stones[1] stretching across 47 wilderness miles of the Pennine hills. It struck me when I first saw the poem 'Snow' that it was similar in its presentation to that of a gravestone, a name followed by an epitaph. The final lines of 'Snow' read:

*'Snow, snow, snow is how the snow speaks, is how its clean page reads.
Then it wakes, and thaws, and weeps.'*

Am I here to thaw, and melt and weep? I'm rather hoping this time will enable me to let some things end and die in order to metaphorically rise to a new life. Stepping out on to the land, offers an opportunity to write a new page.

Figure 3. Stanza Stone 'Snow' at Pule Hill Marsden

---

[1] The Stanza Stones represents 47-mile upland walk, visiting six Stanza Stones carved with poems written by Simon Armitage. It is also the title of a book about the stanza stones, first published by Simon in 2012 with co-authors T. Lonsdale & P. Hall.

Beginnings

My first visit to the Lakes on the 22nd of May at the beginning of this sabbatical was a disaster. I arrived at Rydal Mount, parked, tooled up for the walk and set off determinedly. I was beginning my first walk: an 11-mile round walk with 4,000 feet of ascent. Soon it was raining. As I reached the top of Fairfield Round, as it is best known, I was lost. Everyone who had passed me going down suggested I went with them; my arrogance kept me moving up. I found myself alone, more afraid than I expected ever to be and desperate to return to civilization.

More because of luck than management I picked up a footpath over Cofa Pike meaning I made it down the Fell in the wrong direction and caught the 6.05pm bus out of Glenridding back to Windermere, then a connection to Ambleside followed by a walk back up the A591 to Rydal. The bus ticket was £12.50. The woman at the stop on the other side of the road heading to Penrith was inebriated and friendly. She had been to the pub to watch the football. I was grateful to be back to normal, and in the company albeit briefly of a happy soul!

My original plan was to sleep in Priest's Hole on Heart Crag. Lack of preparation, bad weather and the plain fact that I was not prepared at this stage to be uncomfortable meant I needed to rethink this venture. I learned as I walked on to let this sabbatical unravel as an adventure, and to go easy on myself.

Later that evening I sat in the bus shelter below Rydal Hall, a Christian Retreat Centre, feeling stupid, alone, and weak. I made some supper which included a cup of the grimmest coffee ever. At 2 o'clock in the morning, wrapped in a sleeping bag in my car quite literally having a nightmare I decided to drive home to Yorkshire. My son had sent me a text earlier, 'Dad your sabbatical is not meant to be a "man test" you are meant to enjoy it.'

Arrival

Sweep upwards, here comes the storm bringer!
Thundering below usual altitude rising vertical over crag
travelling at speed robed in cloud and dust
to knock down flat,
arrogance and folly
falling, shot, and gone over the top,
the storm rumbles on
without me.

At the end of my primary education, I found myself on a school trip with classmates staying at the Coniston Youth Hostel. During that week we children hiked around tarns, climbed the Old Man, played rounders, and saw our teachers for the first time as human beings. We also ate oodles of sugary Kendal Mint Cake. I do not remember a happier time in my childhood. I was 11 years old when I was seduced by nature and fell in love with the Lake District.

Over the years I have developed a relationship with the landscape and how nature and people interact with it. As a young adult in the early 1990s, working as a youth worker in Huddersfield, I spent weekends in the Lakes at Chapel Stile providing respite care to foster children. I also spent happy times at Lakeside near Newby Bridge with youngsters from the YMCA youth center in Milnsbridge. These were the halcyon days of my young adulthood, but things were changing.

My personal vocation to ministry was growing and my relationship with the Christian faith was shifting and being challenged. What was God saying? These days were formative, full and abundant. When I married in the mid-1990s, I was keen to share this part of my story, my passion for the fells and lakes, with my wife, and in turn with our now adult children. We have enjoyed many family holidays, often at Easter, walking in the Lakes.

Walking is pleasurable and uplifting. Some of this writing is personally reflective, and some theologically rooted, I am also journaling. No one person is an island, and so I depend on the work of others from whom I occasionally quote.

If there is any originality, it is my poetry. When I say mine, I do not mean that in a possessive sense. Poetry comes to me and if I fail to capture it on the page it is gone, 'On the wind' to quote Bruce Springsteen. He is one of my heroes. Some of these poems arrived crossing fells and in the mountains; others are from other significant times in my life. They capture something that prose simply cannot. They freeze the moment and emotions like a tableau, they become for me a signpost to home.

We all walk on the shoulders of giants. The first giant you will meet is Professor Ivy George. I met her when I was an undergraduate at St John's College. To meet Ivy is to encounter a force of nature. She encouraged me so much whilst in Durham, in life and just before I began this walk.

When my initial plans collapsed, it was her voice that kept speaking to me. Another key voice on this journey was my son, Will, contacting me at the end of that first day. My own flesh and blood arriving in the middle of the night in the form of a text message, speaking directly and explicitly to me.

This sabbatical was a fertile time in my life. I aim to carry forward the lessons of failure and triumph that somehow seemed to manifest themselves during the walking.

It might be helpful for you to know that I have always been a rural parish priest, following a most enjoyable three-year curacy near Leeds with my training incumbent, a Cambridge man, who appeared in my life as a gift to me. Even today, I still chuckle when I think of our Monday morning meetings in the vicarage after Morning Prayer. Michael showed me how not to take myself too seriously, and made my early years of ordained ministry easy. Since those days, I have worked mostly in a team parish context in one of the most beautiful parts of West Yorkshire, the Holme Valley and as a chaplain, first in the Territorial Army now the Army Reserve, both for over 25 years.

This is the first sabbatical 'time out of work' that I have taken. Previous times out of parish ministry were taken working as a military chaplain overseas. Stopping work created space for me to reflect and to be creative, to improve my fitness, diet, and devotional life. I was choosing to make time available to consider what is important at this point in life and in my world. In my reflecting I learnt that one should aim to travel lightly and mostly with optimism. I hope what I discovered mainly about myself reveals itself in the text, but what is true for one person is often a universal truth so I hope this writing will resonate with others also.

Figure 4. The Youth Hostel in Coniston, Yew Pike to the rear

Some of the people who appear in this script have been alongside me for most of my adult life. I have a sense of gratitude for their souls and friendship. Each one of us needs to feel loved. Love is a defining characteristic in the New Testament.

My mother-in-law who left us during the Covid pandemic went out of this world with her eldest and youngest daughter (my wife) physically holding her in their arms, in their love – into 'The habitations of Thy Glory[2].'

Not every life will come to its end this way. My vocation as a Christian priest has placed me alongside people who pass differently. Yet even amid aggressive cancer, the inexorable march of dementia or the madness and violence of war we are unable to deny that deep lament which grows in us when someone we love passes. 'Sorrow and love flow mingled down'[3] such is our compassion. It emotionally and physically hurts not having a corporeal being to direct our love towards when we are forced to bid our last farewell. Inevitably, time displaces the acuteness of such agony.

Presently, I am thinking about death of self, my demise into eternity. Perhaps I am looking forward to a long sleep.

The world at times may appear rancid, and religion may arguably be for some people no more than an unwelcome construct; however, some time ago I came to believing that real life can only be fully experienced when I live by faith. Love has no boundary; it is as bottomless as anyone might ever imagine. The evangelist John points directly to the essence of love. It is 'the way, truth, and life' [John14:6 NIV]. Our forebears were keen to point to the source of such love; any trip around a churchyard memorializes our ancestors.

'God is love, and all who live in love live in God and God lives in them.' [1 John 3:16 NIV]

Those who were willing to accompany me, my friends, blessed me on this journey.

---

[2] John Donne (1572-1631) which pictures the music of heaven.
[3] 'When I survey the wondrous Cross' Isaac Watts (1717).

Walking

In the year 2000, the year of the new millennium, my son stood up and walked for the first time. He wobbled between his mother and I as he took those first teetering steps into his life, and with it his ability to come and go where he might choose began.

I do not remember my first steps, my mother said I walked early. Walking is for most human beings our most natural mode of movement. It is how we get from one place to the other, although we may use aids such as wheelchairs, trolleys, bikes, skis, cars, trains, ships, and planes throughout our lives. Walking is what we do and most of us can do it without thinking. I wear a tracker every day to measure the amount of walking I do. If I fail to make it to the allotted number of steps, I know it has been a bad day at the office, and that most likely the dog is fed up too.

We walk for a variety of reasons ... why am I walking?

In recent memory

I enjoy walking sometimes called hiking which really means a longish but pleasurable demanding walk on trails or footpaths in the countryside. Such walking was especially enjoyable when my wife Sally and I had young children. Because we always had a dog, walks to school were never short, despite the two primary schools our children attended being less than a few minutes' walk away from home. Our walks to school were magical mystery tours through fields surrounded by hedgerows and woods undertaken without fail in all weathers. Someone once said, 'There is no such thing as bad weather, just poor clothing!' On our daily walks we would recite times tables, talk about projects, think about words to describe them, and how to enjoy the day with the other children and teachers.

We would also often bend down or look up to observe nature in its four seasons. The January snow coverings where flowers bloomed last June. We noted tree falls after gusting winds. Our dog would chase the scent of a rabbit or pheasant across a field. Occasionally we would silently steal a look at a deer or stand still and watch a mole scratch and scrabble towards the sunshine. Overhead a squirrel might scamper across the canopy trying to dodge our attention. Snowdrops, crocuses, and bluebells seemed most welcoming as we moved towards the spring term; and mosquitoes, midges and all God's biting insects were most unwelcome on dewy summer mornings. Crispy autumn mornings crinkled under our feet, and the birds would jump out of the hedgerows calling to one another. These early walks to school for me, and I hope for our children, were special. Our daughter Lydia appeared somewhat more adventurous than her elder brother so we two set off in welly boots every day changing them outside the school gates for shiny shoes. For me, these walks were sacred and now much treasured moments in what was then a busy ministry and overly full life.

The School Run

Precious days
when she pulls on the over-covers, and we set sail in the wind,
a blown away moment which will not stay forever:
locked hand in hand, together without a care
we march purposefully to our destination,
weighed down with bags for learning.
Anticipating her future
she gusts at me for knowledge,
Daddy this and Daddy why?
As the dog, sure-footedly pads between us, wagging!
Happy days that speed by whooshing on the wind
as I grab for her small pink hand,
which fits perfectly to mine.
She utters at the gate of arrival before her departure,
'Daddy, I love you.'
A moment later, after the kisses, she skips
to her lessons: hungry for the knowledge within those gates.

As for me and the dog, we pad back to ordinary life and
a bowl of cereal ... knowing that the best part of this day is already gone.

Surprise

My friend Ivy called me from Massachusetts on her last day of term to invite me to visit her in Florida sometime in the future. Before our Zoom chat came to an end Ivy, as positive as ever, exhorted me: 'Sean, when you are crossing the mountains walk right into yourself.'

This was strong advice from one whose opinion I value. One wondered where such encouragement came from given that most of our conversation was about the primary place of Judaism within our understanding of the Christian faith. However, it seemed this was the prophecy I was expected to return to during this sabbatical period.

I do not think that I had considered any notion of walking into myself previously, after all what might this mean? I had, however, considered what walking mountains might entail and as one might expect there was a plan to cross all 214 Wainwright fells in the coming three months. The repetition of walking in an environment which would be changing as I walked through it presented something intangible and unknowable even beyond the physical challenge. I would have the gift of time to do something I enjoy doing whilst at the same time I could reflect on my vocation as a priest and my working life. Was Ivy inviting me to reflect upon what had become of Sean Robertshaw in the time since we last saw each other in Boston some years ago now; and perhaps to go a step further to consider what the future might look like? What is, or might be important and fruitful for the next part of my ministry and life?

Planning

The best planned journeys never quite work out as you might expect. My late friend Don Grayston whilst on pilgrimage in the United Kingdom walking from Land's End to John O' Groats had me pick him up in Glossop, about a 40 minutes' drive southwest of our home. A week later I deposited him in Ilkley some 60 miles further north where he was met by another friend, an American with whom he walked off into the afternoon only to return to our vicarage a few weeks later. I asked Don, 'Did you get to John O'Groats?' 'No,' he replied, 'I got all the way to the Outer Hebrides instead, but I did complete my pilgrimage.'

We took a walk together from Holme Village out to Black Hill in the Dark Peak District. We shared together the story of the Prodigal Son [Luke 15:11-32] told through our own lens and lives. It was for me a deeply confessional moment and as Don prayed for me in the car on the way back all that blackness that sometimes comes over us when we know we have failed to be our best selves seemed to evaporate into the ether. Many times, I have since prayed with people at the end of a walk. And from that time on I took to meeting people for walks when difficult or important things needed to be discussed. Once you get into the rhythm of walking the impossible often seems more possible and the conversation flows more easily. When it gets too tough to keep going one can stop and adjust one's gaze or fix on another topic, discuss what is going on with the weather or use a prop from the environment like a cow or a pathway or a curlew… then pick up the pace again. Walking is non-confrontational. For that reason alone, I decided to make walking my home for this sabbatical.

Following our walk together, throughout the night, I made Don a small icon representing the prodigals' story. He took it back to his home in Vancouver with him.

Pilgrimage or Walking?

In 2018 I submitted a sabbatical application to my employer Leeds Diocese to travel to Assisi. I was going to spend a fortnight with a friend there and then walk to Rome.

These two iconic cities have informed my faith and character in various ways. I had visited them both as a Christian pilgrim previously. So, I was looking forward to journeying between these two places of Christian pilgrimage both of which have been important milestones for me mostly because of past encounters with friends and fellow pilgrims in these cities. They have been places of prayer, reflection, and healing: in Assisi, assisting pilgrims on their journey through the city and in Rome following operational tours with the British Army in both Iraq and Afghanistan.

Complicated work commitments, the changing nature of the Church in Britain, the coronavirus pandemic and a family bereavement caused me to rewrite the 2018 application several times. What eventually emerged was walking the Wainwrights. That is the 214 summits Alfred Wainwright details in his famous *Pictorial Guides to the Lakeland Fells* which he began writing in November 1952 and completed 13 years later.

One of the options which emerged during the planning phase was to walk the mediaeval pilgrim routes – for example St Cuthbert's Way running from Melrose Abbey to Lindisfarne, or the Camino spanning Northern Spain or even The Pilgrims Way from Winchester to Canterbury. All these routes appeared to me immediately seductive yet on this occasion walking in the footsteps of the saints gone before, with them on my mind and their prayers in my heart seemed so far from where I was spiritually. The piety of that thought now makes me balk. This may read oddly, but there was a deep yearning to be away from 'it,' the familiar that is, the Church as an institution.

Now, at the time of writing I recognize that I needed a break from the religious iconography and paraphernalia which for so long had surrounded each day of my life.

Since making that first commitment to Christ at the age of 19 at a Billy Graham rally in Bramhall Lane, Sheffield it had been something of a roller-coaster ride. First joining a church, then working as a youth worker, whilst going back to school and college before training for ordained ministry. Since then, I'd been 'on the job' living out Christian Ministry in West Yorkshire and in other places across the world, sometimes in physically and morally challenging environments.

What I felt was exhausted, weary, and anxious. I felt I needed beauty and nature. Not more Church. I was reminded of Don's adaptability and his ability to be agile and go with the moment and the flow. Work was demanding, change was all around in every area of life, more had to be achieved often with less. I was weary. I needed to close the door and get out. That did not mean I would not come back but hopefully I'd come back better equipped psychologically, feeling more realistic, and ready for the next ten years whatever they might hold. Was I grasping for the tools that would enliven me as I moved towards the future phase of ministry and retirement?

A quote somewhat dubiously attributed to one of my literary heroes Jack Kerouac sometimes credited to his book *The Dharma Bums* reads:

'In the end, you won't remember the time you spent working in the office or mowing your lawn. Climb that goddamn mountain.'

And so that is what I decided to do.

Mountain

Orbit the moon you did.
Dust scattered from space by the hand of knowledge
from the far-flung recess of darkness.
The dawn light breaks over you,
as the sun that spat you out rises in the East.
I will cross you in a day, this day, and the day after.
And all my days… when I am gone and returned to dust
your shape will continue to cast heaven over this earth.

Pruning

Over the years I have climbed many moors, hills, and mountains both literally and figuratively. I grew up in Huddersfield, a northern hill town on the edge of the Peak District in the Pennines. Proudly, I still live there. I wonder will the walking over the next three months begin to heal me from some of those places, people and situations that appeared to have caused me harm and occasionally trauma on my journey over the years of living and ministry?

I want to be clear, I am not looking to blame anyone, it's just that life piles up and when you are busy living it and raising a family there are not so many points to stop and reflect.

Ministry of any kind takes those who deliver it into challenging and often contested situations, ones that are not always easy to resolve. The discipline of daily prayer and weekly biblical reflection in preparation for worship has been immensely helpful in sustaining my faith journey within the wider community. The natural flow of the liturgical year is something I enjoy, especially the worship, particularly at festivals where the parish still seems able to drum up a good congregation.

Whilst preparing for this sabbatical I wondered how stepping away from parish and work and indeed some quite needy and frail people would actually feel? What will leaving them to the love and care of my colleagues bring? I must trust it will work out by the time we arrive at the end of this part of the journey. I will be keen to know if I have made myself redundant. Will anything change for the parishes in terms of ministry. What might I be able to continue to offer? What will become of mission in the parish? And importantly how will God speak as I walk and reflect?

Mountains feature in the Old Testament [e.g., Genesis 22; Exodus 19; 20; 23; 24; 32 and 34. 1 Kings 5; Isaiah 25]. All the epic directions and voices are heard on the roof of the world. This is where God speaks to his chosen servants. In the New Testament too – Jesus heads off to the mountains to pray – to speak and commune with his Father in heaven [Matthew 5; 17; 28. Luke 9:28 etc...] So, I imagine that I stand a fighting chance of encountering God in some way if I walk up into the heights seeking prayerfully the still small voice of calm, the voice that we often sing about in our hymnal, the one that 'Speak[s] through the earthquake, wind and fire.' [1 Kings 19:11-13]

This time of sabbatical will perhaps be most of all a quest to engage in what we are always told as young seminarians ministry is: 'To be and not to do!' Something which is much easier said than done. But I wonder is there more to consider? I mean any life which has been lived in for 50 years or more accumulates clutter. I needed to sort that clutter out, to metaphorically cut it back, prune it out. I want to work out who I have become in a world and in a Church which these days I sometimes struggle to recognize and yet one which requires that I use the gifts, skills, and abilities I have in the care of the community each day. I am after all a Church leader working in a team parish with colleagues.

Figure 5. Clearing in a country garden near Loughrigg Tarn

I am also a chaplain in the Armed Forces in what is a quickly evolving and contested landscape, especially for our Reserve Forces.

There are countless questions about sustainability, the delivery and resourcing of ministry, the Church's mission and how individual Christians and people of faith should engage with their communities, with other faith traditions and secular organizations. In 2004 when the Church of England's 'Mission Shaped' series began its intellectual advance we had not anticipated or lived through and with a pandemic, the wars were not in Europe, but the UK was, and the cost of living was not spiraling out of control as it is now. The landscape of everyone's lives in postmodern Britain is changing, and if I am to continue to be a faith leader I need to evolve and learn to navigate this landscape differently. In the eighteen years since those 'Mission Shaped' publications there has been monumental and unanticipated change. The one clear change for my community is a decreasing need for regular organized faith activities in our local communities. How life-giving is the local church? Given the resources presently available there is a definite practical and spiritual challenge.

So, I have been gifted with three months, maybe more, to do some spring cleaning of mind, soul, and body. Wm. Paul Young in his book *The Shack* uses the imagery of gardening effectively to reflect upon the state of the soul. He suggests '*... It's not the work, but the purpose that makes it special.*' I am aiming to create a clearing, to make space for something new to grow, or at least to cut back what has grown to allow the new shoots to populate the older roots. Stepping away felt daunting but necessary. Making a clearing is hard work, and it often looks messy at the end of the work, but the replanting, time and new growth potentially lead to something new, possibly even fruitful. I wonder, will others be able to accommodate a different version of me?

In Jesus' final sermon to his disciples [John 15:1ff] he uses a gardening metaphor to describe the importance of growing spiritually and the ability to draw strength from him: 'the true vine'. Jesus says, '*He cuts off every branch in me that bears no fruit, while every branch that does bear fruit he prunes, so that it will be even more fruitful.*' [John 15:2 NIV]. Jesus was saying to his followers that he is setting them apart for a lifestyle of bearing fruit. Their fruit would come because of God's intentional pruning. Am I, are we, ever ready to step back from the securities of family, routine, ritual, and the things that make up our days, the comforting and familiar to make a new space? During the sabbatical I moved away from some of the known and familiar.

During the Covid pandemic the deanery clergy were encouraged to attend a trauma workshop. As an introduction to the course we were pointed to Bessel van der Kolk's book *The Body Keeps the Score*. The opening prologue describes various kinds of trauma. I found that I was able to identify with much of what he describes, especially '*human resilience*' which reflects the ability to maintain a stable equilibrium when experiencing trauma. I had at the time of planning guessed that three months of sabbatical were going to be emotionally and morally challenging, being honest with ones-self always is. As I walked, I found myself going into some of those difficult places that over the years have been boxed up on my inside. Matters which I needed to begin to heal from rather than hold in tension, physically and mentally. But like my now dear departed friend Don I aim to complete this journey with an open mind, and with those who are able to join me – with a listening heart, and God willing, fruitfully.

… what am I walking into?

Words

For me words and the way they hang together have always carried powerful resonances and messages. Syntax is king. Grammar is a challenge. Verbs and nouns are friends. Pronouns can be funny and troublesome. Adjectives are sometimes slippery.

The Christmas Gospel from John 1 is deeply textured. In it we discover the eternal Logos, the pre-existent Christ, the eternal and unchanging truth present from the time of creation, is available to every individual who comes searching.

'In the beginning was the Word, and the Word was with God, and the Word was God. [2] He was in the beginning with God. [3] All things came into being through him, and without him not one thing came into being. What has come into being [4] in him was life, and the life was the light of all people. [5] The light shines in the darkness, and the darkness did not overcome it.' [John 1 NRSVA]

For long periods during my adult life, I have striven not to be overcome by darkness, most often particularly characterized for me as anxiety and worry. Thank God for my wife. She is a light bearer to the darkness. Thank you also for those others who understand and have helped keep my torch burning in the middle of what for me can feel like an earthquake.

My working life before Christian ministry and outside the Church has been in environments where language and meaning are visceral, direct, and clear, opposed to the present which is more refined or purposely ambiguous. From 11 years old I worked on a modern productive farm. I learnt how to drive, how to care for animals, how to be pragmatic, how to receive instructions and how to deal with failure and its consequences. Growing up in a northern hill town meant doing a short stint in a textile factory as many others had before me. There was nothing romantic about work, and the pervading attitude from the directors was 'be glad you have a job.' I was just 18, working long hours, hard graft, for poor pay. Above all I respect those who have done this kind of work for much of their lives, men and women like my parents who grew up in the postwar context and knuckled down for their children's future.

More recently, I remember a most quirky Adjutant who would have improved his vocabulary and possibly character by 50% if he could have stopped saying 'fuck', 'fucker' or 'fucking' in every sentence. When I asked him about it, he gleefully told me to, 'Fuck off Padre, it's none of your fucking business.' He called me a 'fucker' under his breath as I left the room. On that occasion I was not traumatized. In fact, I laughed so hard my ribs ached. He intended to have just that effect. They were challenging days: lives were threatened and lost, safety was paramount, laughter was cathartic. He did, however, stop swearing quite so much in front of me from that time on!

Words are powerful – single words, sentences, poems – they bring meaning and insight and capture moments, create curiosity and are active in the use of our imagination. They can and do translate or convey what is perceived by our senses. They communicate feelings and allow us to recite our memories; they open our minds to new horizons beyond the ones we might initially perceive. We are conscious beings. Words are the tools which help us make sense of our lived experience and our humanity. That is our ability to feel, to breathe and to be.

My favourite Shakespearean play by some distance is the tragedy, *Hamlet*. [Act II scene ii]

Polonius: *What do you read, my Lord?*
Hamlet: Words, words, words.

Is the traumatized Prince of Denmark suggesting that words are meaningless without actions? In this brief exchange Hamlet is arguably pointing out that words are tools which we must use to describe human meaning and existence. I am sure that we should be as playful with words as Shakespeare is with his audience, or for that matter the forlorn Hamlet is being with poor old Polonius. The use of repetition here places an emphasis upon the importance of words in relation to the question that has been asked.

I wonder which words I might miss while I am out walking. Will I miss the repetition of leading the church community in the celebration of the Holy Eucharist? I missed the rite during the pandemic as much as I missed the drama. The words may appear simple, but their texture, symbol and meaning are culturally engrained into me, quite literally they are a part of me. The words matter and they are themselves 'the matter'; they conjure up images from the past, in the present and induce a glimpse of the future. Words can present nightmares or visions of hope.

My longtime friend and colleague Steve boldly announced on the journey to a diocesan conference while we were negotiating which lane to be in on the motorway that we should, 'follow the words.' His point was not without irony: he was pointing at a huge sign hanging over the carriageway. We duly moved into the lane marked Liverpool. Words often directly lead us to actions. They instruct us in what to do, and how to do it and words help us to process what we have done and make sense of our actions. Words tell the story.

These words are mostly my words but some of the words belong to others. Some of these words have shaped me; they have shaped me differently to how they will have shaped you. Here you will find mostly, words and stories of regret, of hope, of healing, and of celebration. Words and stories which have joined me on my walks both across Yorkshire and the Cumbrian mountains during my sabbatical.

Some of these stories belong to those others who have been shaped by the landscape in which they lived and worked. I thank them and those who have commented on them for their inspiration to me.

... longing for the fells

Figure 6. Route Card

A good day navigating and walking in Martindale with
Simon. Leaving from Patterdale YHA

> 'Bid thine eye see no further than this blessed
> garden upon which rests the hem of heaven.'
> J. Sean Robertshaw

Figure 7. Ramsden Clough, Holmfirth, a few miles from my home
This ridge is my go-to place

Scout

I realized early that time had changed the context of my walking. I walk almost every day with my dog. He was not going to be present for much of this time. He was becoming too elderly to cover the many miles on consecutive days in the Lakes. He would join me on a few of the occasions but in my heart, I knew I would miss his company, observations, and wayfinding. Perhaps memory will help me to be mindful of him as I walk.

Dogs often appear with walkers and travellers: The writer John Steinbeck in *Travels with Charlie* (1961) devoted much of his writing to his companion 'Charles Le Chien', a Bleu poodle born and trained on the outskirts of Paris who spoke only in French and was by profession a diplomat, chiefly because he was bad at fighting.

Dogs are good travelling companions. No, I am wrong, dogs are the best of companions. As I sit editing these notes in early winter at a lodge in the Lakes Scout is asleep at the side of me. He accompanied me to the top of Hartsop Dodd from Brother's Water this morning, even though he is aged he still moved over the land like flowing ink, ranging out then coming back to show me the way. Ever faithful, ever courageous, forever the Ranger! My resting heart rate is lower when I am relaxed with Scout.

All my life I have had a dog, even when I was at university, I walked a tutor's dog. You cannot own a dog and fail to walk. Dogs love walking, running, jumping, swimming, and fetching. Dogs are fun and indeed like human beings they need exercise for their wellbeing. For a dog it is a world of smells, and their joy just seems to overflow walking across open fields, running in woods, or hunting on the moors.

My present dog, Scout, is my second Labrador Retriever and friend. He's too old now to walk the big walks but the daily few miles and swims in the local reservoirs are a joy to us both whatever the weather, alone or with others. Scout wags his tail at foe and friend alike, forever optimistic that in this approaching creature a playmate might be found.

Scout requires little direction from us; he watches our every move. We are his pack and so he knows when to wait, when to interrupt, when to speak. Yes speak! If you have ever owned a dog, you might have a voice that you use for it.

We anthropomorphize Scout; it is as if he were one of us. When we do not use his voice Scout speaks to us through his presence. This way of speaking is significant. What he smells and observes we do too when we are paying attention. When we leave the house on our morning walk if the roe deer are in the woods, he tells me long before we see them. If someone comes to the bottom of the vicarage driveway, he moves quickly towards them. If we are not in sight, he calls out with a growl and loud bark and then struts around looking important until we arrive. When we do, he wags his tail endlessly and advances to the new and interesting smell, which is usually someone arriving.

Scout is like our shadow. He is never far from our consciousness, love, and attention. His desire is simply to be with us, in our presence. Most mornings he comes into our bedroom, hunts for a sock, and brings it to us in his soft mouth, tail wagging: 'Come on it's time for a walk,' he's saying. Get your socks on!

In Retirement

Paws pad, claws track back.
Your black faithful wag presents this moment.
You lead to the head of the track then break for the gate
where the years now condemn you to wait. I will go ahead for a while.
You sit in discontent as I disappear into the fell where we once roamed together.
Raising your nose to the wind you listen to my heartbeat and sense my presence, now far from sight your intelligence pierces the distance.
Even in your absence my imagination glimpses you flowing like oil over peat and craggy outcrops.
Flushing a cock pheasant, running at a rook; heeling past lowland sheep; over moor and fell we have travelled together.
I will track back to you.

Figure 8. Scout near the peak of Wansfell Pike 1,597 feet

'I am walking into myself; nothing is behind me; I am akin to an open pathway. No ties in this moment bind me.'

Friendships

My friend Angus who now lives in British Columbia is a near perfect travelling companion, low maintenance. We can communicate without speaking and often do. We move at different speeds but together. The last time I saw him was in Chiswick. I parked at Kew (beyond the emission and parking zones) and walked down the side of the River Thames. I was walking towards a 30-year friendship, one which is divided by the Atlantic Ocean and nearly 4,600 kilometers of inhospitable land mass. This meeting took place at the end of the pandemic. We had not seen each other for two years barring the odd Skype call. The last time we met was in Assisi where we walked the Rieti Valley in Umbria, following in the footsteps of the sainted Brother Francis.

There have been other times when we have walked together following the footsteps of those pilgrims gone before. In the mountains of the Okanagan, through the desert of Nevada, in the streets of New Orleans, in the pine forests of Vancouver; across the three peaks of the Yorkshire Dales, in Northumbria and County Durham under the cathedral spires where we met whilst at university. Two sometimes reluctant Anglican priests travelling together to listen, observe and live by walking obediently in the footsteps of the others they are listening to. In the presence of the Spirit which lives in all things, the quiet presence of life itself.

Figure 9. Rev Dr Angus Stuart drinking coffee. Chiswick 2021

Durham City

There is some convergence
life and Spirit melt into one here.
There is some respectability in these atoms.
Some divine spark expressed by humanity.
The architecture like the conversation is austere,
divided block by block, stone by stone.
Carefully thought out, processed, fine-tuned, chiselled by dialogue.

Perseverance is a quality expressed on paper,
in an idea – through quick-witted articulation.

The conversation like the eye is directed in this city into eternity.
Look, this is where bare-breasted humanity with little humility grafted into
the ground its own 'Spirit'.
Five towers reaching heavenwards rising into the celestial darkness, illuminated each night by human endeavor.
Lord God, this day which we have inhabited,
we bow our knees, close our eyes, and pray:
bring me like the eye closer to your heart.
Amen.

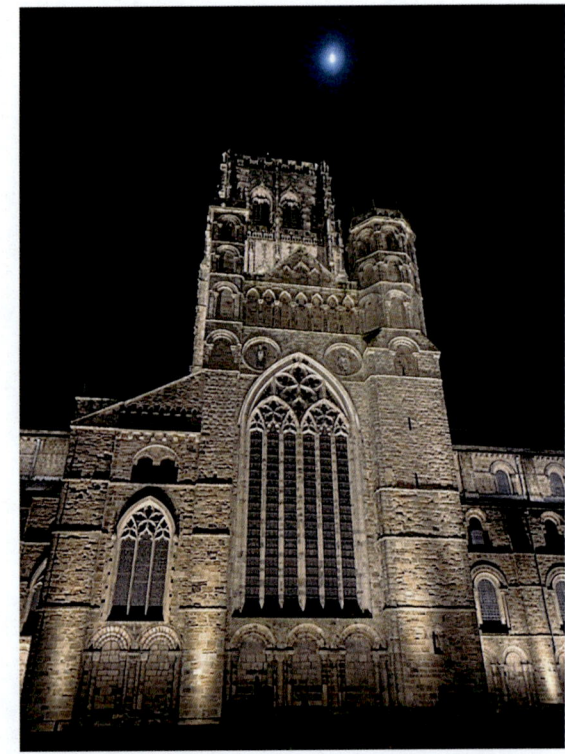

Figure 10. Durham Cathedral photographed at night

Friendship is important. I quickly discovered that it wasn't good for me to be alone too often while crossing the high fells, especially in bad weather without a dog. I have often enjoyed being alone and in my own company but on this occasion, it just wasn't working. I felt the need to be with others who I trusted but for whom I didn't have to take responsibility. I quickly thought of people I could invite to walk with me some of whom had already said they would enjoy a day walking in the Lakes.

Figure 11. Sarah Branson leading a felt-making workshop in the church community garden

Friendship with the earth is important too. The earth keeps us and sustains us; it is life itself and without it and its processes we are surely doomed. Our human record is not that great when we consider how we each care for the source that sustains us physically. My friend Sarah cares for the earth. She is an environmental artist and forest school leader. Sarah values the resources nature offers us. She creates beautiful landscape images made from felt, uses fire in her workshops and leads mindfulness sessions in the church Community Garden. Sarah epitomizes harmony and reality. Spirituality and goodness flow from her but importantly she has a determined and gritty edge that authenticates her artistry. I have never seen Sarah in any footwear other than walking boots. Sarah is always dressed to walk into the outdoors or into life.

Rain

When it begins to rain in the Cumbrian mountains, which it surely does on most days, the mountains begin to flow: the flowing water appears as like silver being poured out of the ground. The gills, waterways and streams come to life across the fell and fall in one endless torrent into the valley floor, moving ever downward into the rivers and tributaries which eventually run into the sea. The water which gathers in pools on the fells above the tarns and lakes is golden and peaty. It glistens when the sun comes out. If you dip your arm into the water it turns to gold and when you withdraw it, like magic, it is as fresh as before. 'I am the light of the world,' says Jesus [John 8:12] ... when we befriend the earth, we walk into the light which strikes the earth and animates it.

James Newcome, Bishop of Carlisle, when opening the refitted water-driven turbine which provides electricity for the diocesan retreat center Rydal Hall commented that, *'The one sure sustainable in the Lake District is the Cumbrian rain.'*

Figure 12. Rain flowing in tributaries down the Fell sides

Figure 13. Flowing water: the beck falling through Ashness Bridge near Keswick

Even in the rain walking can be an occasional delight. It might seem odd to write about befriending elements of the creation but, when crossing the fells, peaks and lakes, chronological time stretches from the far distant past. When combined with one's sense of awe and mystery there is always in vision an awareness of eternity, and our small part in it, and a growing responsibility to take care of it while we live out our time in it.

Creation forever presents the new: a bud, a flower, a fungus, insects, birds, deer, stoats, and lizards to name but a few of the things I've bumped into whilst walking. Often it is just a flashing glimpse and no more. A moment which arrives like an unexpected gift. A revelation of something known but unforeseen. An occasion that often takes your breath away and fills you with joy.

The land changes; so does the weather and likewise the seasons. The land sustains the life of thousands of creatures. As I crossed these landscapes, I was occasionally aware of Brother Francis in my consciousness. When finding himself with no congregation he decided to preach to the birds in Bevagna and he also befriended a wolf in Gubbio thus saving the townsfolk from its appetite. I have not felt the need to preach to the fells, but I imagine they are speaking to me of the eternal as I cross their many miles. Their freshness fills me with a sense of goodness and awe. I feel I am being filtered and cleansed like the water that flows through them.

Psalm 150:6 reminds us that all things in creation have a purpose *'Let everything that has breath praise the Lord,'* [NIV] and Psalm 66:4 reminds us of our place within the created order: *'All the earth bows down to you.'* [NIV]. God's handiwork does not need me to speak for it; it has an independent life of its own. My responsibility is to care for it, protect its treasure, and cherish it for future generations.

> **'It is no use walking anywhere to preach unless our walking is our preaching.'**
>
> *Brother Francis of Assisi*

Company

John O'Donohue writes in *Eternal Echoes*, 'Hearing an echo in the lonely landscape of the mountains seems to suggest that we are not alone that we belong here on this earth ... Our hunger to belong is the longing to bridge the gulf that exists between isolation and intimacy.'

I am most grateful for the company of family and friends who joined me walking in the Lake District. Also, for fellow travellers I met on mountainsides, campsites and in youth hostels. And the hospitality of the indigenous Lakeland folk. I soon discovered during those early days of walking that being alone might appear romantic but was anything but that! One's mind can wander into unhelpful recesses.

Figure 14. Catkins through winter snow

Each fellow-walker has brought me some wisdom and a thought that has inspired or challenged me. Other companions have sometimes appeared in my imagination much like Marley in Dickens' *A Christmas Carol*.

As one walks and reflects not only the natural scenery flows through one but also other scenes from life come to mind. Walking is rhythmical and it helps me to reflect upon and ruminate over these scenes from my past whilst crossing the fell. As one walks conversations can thaw and open like the catkins in the earliest days of spring.

Thoughts can be inspiring, even heroic, other times difficult when perhaps facing failures, big decisions, or dealing with worries about health, work, or relationships; or when reflecting inwardly on attitudes, and people past and present. When we walk, we walk into the world and into life.

Depending upon our starting point we might have very different expectations and aspirations as we take our journey through life. I am aiming to be optimistic as I walk forward into the next phase of life. Perhaps it is time to begin considering one's death. 'Dust you are, and to dust you shall return.' [Genesis 3:19]. As I walk these fells there are comforting tones in these words.

The massive mountains which border the Lakeland valleys might be representative of the kinds of conversations we have with the others past and present, within ourselves or with the Holy Spirit.

Those big questions that reoccur from time to time: why, who, when and what?

A day out walking can bring a great deal of insight to bear upon self, our relationships, the questions we face and the issues we struggle with in our own communities and increasingly across the world. I have discovered that walking slows one down and brings the whole of life into clearer perspective. It has been well documented that walking is not only physically good to do, but that it is good for our mental well-being too.

Walking

Woken early by the chattering buntings and chaffinches
I spy my four black toes and feel the throb of aching limbs,
stinging eyes and sun-burnt forearms
storm damage written on this flesh.

Walking over crag and high fell
reaching high into the sky.
Sun, rain, drifting drizzle and cloud.
They change your clothes, your life, your mind.

Wet and sodden, wringing boots
down the mountain track and back to Patterdale.
Squelching pathways, tree roots cover the earth.
The birds are busy ringing in new birth.
The sleeping mat and black warm cap
crawl into a bunk with a steaming cup
too exhausted to eat supper.
Tomorrow will offer more stone
to climb the fells in flesh and bone.

Many have walked this way
with time to watch to live and pray.

Crossing vast landscapes or walking directly up for 2,500 feet or more requires a kind of detachment from the body. Why? Because the brain is crying out for oxygen which in turn produces the energy our muscle needs when doing arduous exercise. The brain independently takes control of our bodily functions. Our heart rate increases, we start to sweat, breathing becomes more laboured. Walking is demanding. Exercise is good for us physically; it extends our life expectancy. It is better to walk than exist in a relatively sedentary state.

Walking off Troutbeck Tongue on one of the hottest days in living memory in the British summer required an immediate reassessment of my bodily and topographical situation. Such scrutiny demanded that I called to mind choices and the tools I had available to survive the three-kilometre trek, under a raging sun along the valley floor back to my shelter.

Heat injury is something much misunderstood. It is, however, serious and can lead to death. Again, I had underestimated the task I had set myself, walking from Jesus Church in Troutbeck up over Sour Howes on to Sallows and then down on to Troutbeck Tongue. By eleven o'clock I had downed nearly three litres of water. The aim was to climb out from the valley floor and take the steep upwards climb to Baystones to finish on Wansfell Pike overlooking Ambleside. In total approximately 3,623 feet of ascent and the same back down. I dipped out under the shade of a tree by Trout Beck, refilled my water bottle in the bubbling waters and left Baystones and Wansfell to the following day. I was learning to be pragmatic and flexible, and to be generous to myself, to listen to the elements and my body, to foster and debate realistic expectations.

No one here was judging my performance. No one knew where I was or what I was doing: I was free from expectation.

Being able to walk offers those who can endless new horizons.

Firstly, when we walk recreationally or out of a sense of happiness time seems to pass at a different speed. Walking is measured in distance travelled rather than as chronological events.

Secondly, when high on the fell (when there is no cloud cover) the low-lying land and valley bottom is seeable. So, for example, a bird's-eye view from the top of Illgill Head in Wasdale reveals the glory of the valley below, and looking out to the northeast you can see beyond the coastline of Cumbria across the Irish Sea all the way to Dumfries and Galloway.

When walking on the high fell stopping and taking a view is simple, just move your gaze towards the place you are intending on moving into, through or past. It makes good sense. Maps can give us a great deal of detail but seeing the land is often awe inspiring. Looking feeds memory, which also has an important part to play as we reconstruct the landscape in our mind's eye. When we cross fells and mountain peaks, we can examine it in detail as Alfred Wainwright did. Alternatively, we can pass over with a more generalist glance. By the time you are returning down the mountain, the time, weather, even feelings concerning relationships may have been tested or changed.

Walking in the Northern Fells across Skiddaw and Blencathra on sheet shale slate deposits which were once under a pre-historic ocean and are now 3,000 feet high in the sky is literally a breathtaking thought.

Alternatively, in Borrowdale the huge slabs and rocks have erupted out of the volcanic land mass. When considered it looks as if it happened only yesterday. When stooping to drink from the high-lying tarns a legacy from the ice age you begin to gain perspective on the now, on the present, the tangible, and the work of creation and evolution. Five hundred million years ago these mountains were in their infancy. They came from a different place and ended up here.

The closing chapters of Job echo in mind as I walk…

'Where were you *Sean* when I…?'

Then the LORD spoke to Job out of the storm. He said:

2 "Who is this that obscures my plans with words without knowledge?
3 Brace yourself like a man; I will question you, and you shall answer me.
4 "Where were you when I laid the earth's foundation?
　Tell me, if you understand.
5 Who marked off its dimensions? Surely you know!
　Who stretched a measuring line across it?
6 On what were its footings set, or who laid its cornerstone—
7 while the morning stars sang together, and all the angels shouted for joy?
8 "Who shut up the sea behind doors when it burst forth from the womb,
9 when I made the clouds its garment and wrapped it in thick darkness,
10 when I fixed limits for it and set its doors and bars in place,
11 when I said, 'This far you may come and no farther;
　here is where your proud waves halt'?

Job 38:1-11 [NIV]

'And my feet...'

I often imagine Peter, James, and John walking with Jesus across the various mountains and hills around Jerusalem. Jesus heads off to the top without them. They are playing catch up. They are always playing catch up, so are we! 'Do we wait here? Do we go with him? Will he return this way?' I can almost feel their concern. Mostly Jesus asks that they stop and pray.

Whilst walking the fells I often felt compelled by the forces of nature or the weight of faith to bow down to touch the earth, look up and pray, and to give thanks for all that is good and wholesome and undefeated and unbroken in our beautiful world.

So often our church intercessions lead us to pray for all those things that really are not of the kingdom of God nor ever were. At the heart of sin is our own failure, yet even so God the Son sets out to rescue us. Why do we list our failures in our worship? Human sin is tragic yet by faith we trust that the battle over death is already won. It could be remiss not to review those attitudes and behaviours that belong to the earth and to humanity, those things that remind us of our failure to care for the world or the people in it. However, our prayers surely must aim to capture a restored vision of the earth, not echo a broken one.

When we walk into nature there are signs of beauty and tenderness all around us. I was staggered one day whilst ascending Loughrigg Fell from the iridescent tarn below. I captured a picture of heaven: sheep and their lambs on the lowlands, families swimming in the quiet waters, people perambulating slowly in the sun across the green grass and wooded hillsides, birds, butterflies and dragonflies in abundance and the most delicate and beautiful flowers all in bloom. I sent a friend who has graced my life with kindness and beauty a text. It read, 'Today I am contemplating beauty.' Honestly, there was little choice. It was my walking companion.

'Walk upon England's Pleasant Land'
Lord, you are the author of all that is and all that will be.
Let your kingdom come and come and come
praying that your will is done.
Help us humbly to receive our daily portion
and give you praise for the beauty of creation. Amen.

I am guessing that others have stopped to pray in these places before; many a cairn, seat, or way-marker along the footpath in the Lakeland mountains memorializes someone who was loved by their family and friends. A person who in life passed this way or that and for some personal reason was acquainted with the place in which they presumably have asked to be remembered. Was this their portion of heaven on earth?

**Figure 15. Orrest Head summer 2022
Alfred Wainwright's first view of the Lakeland fells 1932**

The view from Orrest Head just above Windermere is the first view that Alfred Wainwright had of the Cumbrian Mountains in 1932. The view into the Langdale Pikes and beyond is truly inspiring and surely it captured his imagination and passion. Almost every inch of what he saw on that day he documented as routes thereof in detail. Although his ashes were deposited in Innominate Tarn as he requested, perhaps this is the one place in which he is best remembered by his fans and followers. This is where his journey began; it was no less than a love affair. His books to this day inspire others who share that same passion of walking in the Cumbrian mountains. This was where I finished my sabbatical period, looking out, and into the places I had walked, wistfully gazing out across the fells I had crossed.

There is a deep memory in the land. The Cumbrian farmer and writer James Rebanks in his book *A Shepherd's Life* reminds the reader that the sheep are hefted to their ancestral fells. Meaning they belong there. They know their territory and their land, where to find shelter, grazing and fresh water. They know the sound of the farm machinery and the call of the shepherd as he or she arrives to tend to them. If the farm is sold the sheep are sold with it for they alone know truly the dimensions of their pastures.

Rebanks himself makes reference to Alfred Wainwright and his lovingly crafted Lakeland guide books which continue to attract cult-like status among those of us like me who are 'Wainwright baggers' (which Alfred himself would disapprove of) but there is something poignant in Rebanks' detailed observation.

> *'They are beautiful, thoughtful little books and exert a powerful hold on how other people see our landscape. They cast a spell over my teachers at school, whose entire perception of the Lake District was shaped by these handful of books…It struck me powerfully that there was scarcely a trace of any of the things we cared about in what Wainwright had written…In my bones I felt it did matter. That seeing, understanding and respecting people in their own landscapes is crucial to their culture and ways of life being valued and sustained.'*
>
> *The Shepherd's Life: A Tale of the Lake District.* James Rebanks

Whilst walking the high fells of Martindale I noticed that there were newly erected fences dividing up parts of the land. I understand now that this is part of a re-wilding scheme, an attempt to turn back towards the old lore and a way of farming which means managing the land differently, respecting it and not exploiting its resources to excess.

The fells of Martindale are not only a home to sheep but also to red deer. Walking over Rest Dodd gives access to a permissive path on which The Nab appears before you as a dome below. Crossing the saddleback between the two high points is peaty and wet underfoot. Access although not forbidden is discouraged. I recall carefully descending Nab End, a steep route, not much used, down to Dale End pausing to watch the red deer contentedly resting on the fells in the mid-afternoon. Red deer such as these appeared 11,000 years ago, when they came to Britain from Europe; their meat, hides and antlers provided our ancestors with an important source of food, clothing, and tools. With the development of agriculture much of the deer's natural habitat was destroyed, meaning red deer disappeared from many parts of England. Only one herd of pure-bred red deer remains in England. It is in the Martindale Deer Forest. These creatures are a living signpost and a beautiful one at that, of something our forebears would depend upon to sustain their very lives. Their natural habitat, the land!

Celebration

I have walked in celebration of creation. The awe and wonder of the land and seascapes caused me oft times to pause and consider with the psalmist the opening verses of Psalm 19:1-4 [NIV]

1 *The heavens declare the glory of God;*
  the skies proclaim the work of His hands.
2 *Day after day they pour forth speech;*
  night after night they reveal knowledge.
3 *Without speech or language,*
  without a sound to be heard,
4 *their voice has gone out into all the earth,*
  their words to the ends of the world.

In the Parish of St Peter, Martindale I discovered a church full of inspiring stained glass; such beauty had been curated there over many generations. The west end of the church takes for its theme the Benedicite, Omnia Opera Domini in English '*All ye works of the Lord, bless the Lord.*' colloquially known as the Song of Creation. I wonder was it the same matter Brother Francis of Assisi had in mind when he composed the Canticle of the Creatures.

Brother Francis believed God is Our Father (Abba), and he pointed to familial relationships within God's creation through this canticle. Birds, fire, and wind are brothers. The moon, stars and water are sisters and planet Earth who nourishes us is Mother. Creation is nature viewed with the Creator in mind; creation is fullness, life, and community. Creation's end is unity. The canticle expresses a wish for such unity, offers praise, gives thanks and reveals a great love for God.

Following a retreat in Assisi amongst the congregants of St Francis in the Wood from British Columbia I was presented with a beautiful mosaic with the words of the canticle painted onto it. This is something I treasure. It reminds me of a season and of the generosity not only of those pilgrims but indeed the greater generosity of God which is freely evidenced in our relationships with one another and the creation. I remember one evening after sharing the Eucharist and dining together, one of the pilgrims, a dance teacher, began to dance. We all joined in. The movement was joyous and easy. The spontaneity of this event was a demonstrative thanksgiving for the goodness we were experiencing building friendships, trading stories, and living and walking in the footsteps of the Sainted Francis. I think if Francis were speaking directly to us now, we would hear how he implicitly grasped that all life is intimately connected with God's creation. God's invention is all around us and we are each a part of it. The divine invitation is to step deeply into its activity and to become one with it. Being human is special and is to be celebrated. Whilst walking across the fells it has been easy to look up to the heights or down into the valleys with a sense of awe. When I feel the wind blowing upon my face, I am mindful that the Holy Spirit is entirely present.

Topping Out (*reaching the top of a peak*)

The ascent to the top of Black Crag to gain access over Blencathra is hindered today by a strong wind. The door is blown shut on our intended ascent. So, rather than scrub out our lives by ignoring the weather, or possibly incurring the embarrassment of calling the Mountain Rescue because of a fall off Sharp Edge we walk the leeward way up the fell from Mungrisdale over Souther Fell and ascend the less prominent exposure.

The wind is still driving, and each step forces my effort. My lungs are aching to release the carbon dioxide built up in my body – the toxin slows my climb. I am unable to defy the force of nature and my physiology conspires to bring me to stand still. I stop to ponder the landscape. I'm moving across and up some 2,847 feet of a vast mountain scape. The not so gentle wind is in my face and chest. The walking requires effort, it is beautiful.

Figure 16. Blencathra from Mungrisdale Common

Awe assails me. I relax my gaze to look across from a rocky path towards the foreground and beyond. I see the distant summit. *'Be still and know I am God,'* Psalm 46:10 [NIV] reverberates in my mind. I walk again and the distance closes as I move into it. I am with an experienced mountaineer whom I trust: he will not suffer my foot to slip or stumble – *'He watches over my going out and coming in'*. I am reflecting on words from Psalm 121 [NIV]. This friendship has a special potency for me. It has been built over many years through youth, early adulthood, and family connections. We have together walked fell, hill and mountain. Whether climbing or caving the years have galvanized a bond of trust between us and a wisdom to know how to read the signs and portents surrounding us. We have nothing to prove. We are both looking into the next part of our lives. I am watching my friend cut a solitary route through the fell. I'm hanging behind to allow us both to be. There is no defeat in adapting one's route to the weather conditions or to the constraints of older bodies, and greater familial and professional responsibility. Upon reaching Blencathra's summit we take the long fall off across Mungrisdale Common to Cloven Stone which stretches out in a westerly direction below us... Why, Alfred Wainwright, did you want us to walk this way? Upon tuning round at the cairn, it was obvious this view of the mountain is surely one of the best and least observed.

... Rain clouds are gathering I must make it soon to the top... I rather think I need to reach the top to see what the falling is all about... I'm still walking Ivy.

Crossing Out

On my desk is a rugged wooden cross. I made it in 2017 during a week of mission in the local valley churches. This was during the summer before our son William was to leave home and move to Glasgow to begin a five-year degree course. I chatted to a fellow missionary in the church Community Garden. I expressed my concerns and anxieties about my son leaving home and indeed his ability to survive away from us.

The small crudely constructed cross I made that day has remained on my desk in a prominent place since and has acted as a signpost to remind me to pray for him. That first day of travel, one which I guess many parents have experienced with a car full of homely items to be deposited in the halls of residence, wasn't emotionally easy. Neither did the Wolfson residential block fill me with the sense of awe I first experienced as an undergraduate in Durham under the Cathedral spires. Our son was almost as big as the tiny room we deposited him in. The most difficult day of my life had arrived. We had to leave him. I had to leave him, and trust others would care for him.

Our 14-year-old daughter greedily ogled the sites and appeared already more set for freedom than him. I would have almost been happier to leave her. She somehow seemed more equipped for independence. Lydia is uncomplicated; everybody appears to love her, and people naturally move towards her. Her laughter and happiness are infectious. Now all this may appear absurd, after all do not all parents want their children to grow in stature and independence and learn to face new challenges? Of course, we do! Kahlil Gibran comments in his work *The Prophet*:

> *'Your children are not your children.*
> *They are the sons and daughters of Life's longing ...*
> *You may house their bodies but not their souls ...*
> *You are the bows from which your children as living arrows are sent forth.'*

I had left them before to walk in Canada with my friend, to cross the USA on more than one occasion, and to go with the British Armed Forces to some of the most kinetic operations that have taken place in the last 20 years. This leaving '*him*' felt somehow different. I wasn't in control and felt unable to marshal my emotions. Before we abandoned our son to the mercy of yet unknown peers and a new life, we went to scope out the geography which included a look around the buildings he would be studying in. Above the doorway through which he would pass most days I noticed the university motto written in Latin: 'Via, Veritas, Vita.' '*Way, Truth, Life.*' [John 14:6 NIV]. Somehow this penny had not dropped in the slot sooner, (no surprise there). It was as if God were speaking directly to me. 'He's safe here, he's with me; I'll never leave him or you.' And so in faith we left him in his tiny room anticipating a return journey in two weeks' time to move him out and bring him home. We never had to make that journey, rather we marvelled at the life he made socially, emotionally and intellectually. He walked into his dreams. Dreams have a way of working in us and through us. Without dreams there is no hope.

During the sabbatical we spent a fantastic weekend in Glasgow. We worshipped with St Mary's Episcopal Cathedral congregation and attended our son's graduation ceremony and the graduation ball. A celebration in Caledonia is always going to be a good one. Music, bagpipes, dancing, and song, hugging and joy. A moment of happiness, of meeting and of lament. The ball at the Armadillo appeared like a scene from CS Lewis' book, The Last Battle in which everyone had to be hugged for we will not all be here tomorrow to hug in this way again.. Sally and I wobbled on foot the few miles back to our hotel hand in hand and happy.

'The term is over: the holidays have begun. The dream is ended: this is the morning.' C.S. Lewis, *The Last Battle*

The Graduation

Waiting for the last time in this line,
now versed intimately in the alumni: frocks, kilts, and suits.
That new look; a hidden fatigue, new wisdom and anticipation.
Five hundred miles moved and gone, and all too soon it will be time to go again.

The vice-chancellor honours your cohort. Graduates doff caps,
whilst you smile nervously waiting for your name to be called.
Applauding politely,
it's your turn in the line of prospecting new hopefuls.
Adrenaline, ego, fear a heady mix as you stride smiling to the call.

Leaving is crossing your consciousness even
whilst this pageant infuses you.
A whole lifetime cannot undo this moment;
rather friendship will wrap it in nostalgia.

A square mile of West End life at an end.
A lament for a tenement flat and friends.
A tested wrap of safety bonds dissolved for a later time.

It is not easy growing into the robes that adorn you today, or their
expectations that give rise to yet unknown hidden depths of being.

The bronze flash on your shoulder shines like your freshness.
Like armour it will protect you if you trust its provenance.
The joy of today will fly the colours of triumph tomorrow.

If ideas desert you, or you this life,
if there is no known way to go then truth abides.
Adorned in the academy and spotlighted brightly today.
Tomorrow you will all be scattered to season the world.

Graduates don't forget your childhood, don't forget how to play.
Carpe Diem.

Figure 17. The Science Centre (aka The Armadillo), Glasgow

Back in the Lakes – Wasdale

I spent the beginning of the week in Wasdale camping with two friends. The banter was funny, male, and easy. It was a pleasure to be there sharing this time with others who were well-organised and made camping funny ha ha. We erected three tents (this sounds familiar – Matthew 17:4?), ate lunch and set off down the eastern bank of Wast Water, eventually crossing the boulder screes. It was hot, difficult walking and after 4 miles we turned southeast to ascend the fell. Straight up following the flow of Greathall Gill then a break left onto Whin Rigg at 1,755 feet. Whilst there we were blessed by a double flyby of a peregrine falcon, majestic, wild and beautiful. We crossed the fell in a northeasterly direction to the slightly higher peak of Illgill Head before arriving quite exhausted after a steep descent back at the camping site which also sported a pub! Showers were available as was beer, so we cut to beer, laughter, and food before bed. The weekend was fun and included an impromptu swim in Wast Water and a trip to the top of Hard Knott (Another Wainwright bagged for me, 1,803 feet.). My companions in true

'Summer Wine[4]' fashion played their parts nobly and with true dedication. As they left me at Wasdale Head campsite my ribs ached only slightly more than my head.

Walking in Wasdale offers the highest of the Lakeland mountains. Wasdale, even when busy, seems to have a dominant, uninterrupted silence about it. Sited in the western part of the Lake District arguably this is the most rugged and spectacular of places. The journey to the valley head is nearly four miles long at the end of a thin, winding, narrow piece of tarmac which snakes along the valley floor following along the west bank of Wast Water, England's deepest lake. Directly in front of you, north, stands the titan called Great Gable, a single rock raised from the ground which resembles the shape of a fighting Dane's helmet. To the east Lingmell, Scafell Pike and Scafell, England's highest mountains, flanked by Middle Fell to the west and Illgill Head southeast. You feel as though you are entering an Amphitheatre made for drama and indeed if you are here to climb 'prepare ye self' for the encounter and the euphoria of the ascent.

At the head of Wasdale, is a Church dedicated to St Olaf. It is rumoured to be the smallest church in England, roofed with huge slate tiles over beams that came from wrecked Viking ships.

A Visitor

Mike has a guardsman's moustache although he is a Padre. Mike is one of the most understated, kindest, and most generous persons I have ever met. We have become over the years of our ministries good and trusted friends. Mike offered to come walking with me months ago when we were running a course together in Shrivenham at the Defence College.

I seized on the opportunity to invite Mike to walk with me in Wasdale. He is fit, a competent map reader and most importantly great company. Mike is like a spaniel full to the brim with ideas and he is always positive. His optimism is rooted in his personal and committed relationship with Jesus. He is a *'true Israelite'* [John 1:47] and an inspiration to me. Possibilities are endless in Mike's world and he is a great touring companion, never indecisive and always on point. He can turn out a brew kit at the top of a mountain with time to idle. Mike is a great version of Jesus, one of the best I have met. Planning with him is easy: you say what your aim is; he miraculously does the rest in his way. I'm usually happy to go with the flow. As I previously indicated, we all walk on the shoulders of giants. Mike has that rare gift of being able to turn water into wine [John 21-11] in other words he can seemingly work miracles!

---

[4] A long running sitcom TV series set in my home town of Holmfirth, in the Holme Valley. written by Roy Clarke and originally broadcast by the BBC from 1973 to 2010.

When Mike arrived in Wasdale I was at my campsite at the northwesterly end of the lake, tenting in the pub field. Mike had agreed to arrive at 1730. He did eventually arrive in his red VW California camper two hours later than planned. As usual he had the biggest grin on his face ever seen. It was a delight to see him, the two hours went unmentioned. We went to the pub for supper. Then having struck my little camp we jumped in his van and set off to a better than average seasoned travellers' campsite in Nether Wasdale, one Mike had booked. It had toilets and showers, much appreciated by me. We then settled in for the night before rising early to head back down the lake to begin our walk up Lingmell, Scafell Pike, Scafell and Slight Side. Such a day takes in more than 4,000 feet of ascent and covers some of the most testing routes in the English Lakes. We were quickly and early out the blocks powering up Lingmell into the low-lying cloud before crossing over onto Scafell Pike, the highest English summit standing at 3,209 feet. Although up early we were not there alone.

Visibility was at best sketchy as we peered bleary-eyed through the occasional break in the cloud. Navigation was not easy either. For the unfamiliar, the top of Scafell Pike resembles a moon landing scene. It is pretty much all rock. The polished and shiny rocks represent many years of footfall and the occasional and sporadic walkers' cairns point the way, but which way? This mountain has over 100 visitors most days of the year. There is a well-trodden path almost equivalent to a motorway which leads the hordes the top and back, but walkers should never underestimate mountains and certainly not this one. It is deceptively dangerous in poor weather and one's bearings in cloud and mist are easily lost.

Figure 18. View through the cloud on Scafell

We arrived at the summit and dutifully took our place in the line to stand on the viewing ledge constructed since I was last atop this peak. Mike was on his phone arranging a funeral. The weather steadfastly remained poor, so we moved into the small shelter, brewed up and had a bite before negotiating the way over to Scafell.

Neither of us wanted to risk life or limb so having crossed Mickledore we descended to a chimney that in winter I assume is the gill which overflows Foxes Tarn. Then we climbed assuredly up to what must be the smallest tarn in the Lake District and on from there up to the top.

By now the visibility had improved significantly and we could look back across to clearly see Scafell Pike. This was a mountain peak I would later in my walking keep picking out from the skyline. We brewed a cup of tea, ate some flapjack, and sat on the fell-side enjoying the view through the mountains and across the Irish Sea out as far as the Isle of Man.

The next part of our walk meant following the natural ridge south to bag Slight Side, our final and perhaps for me the most surprising peak, lower than Scafell and Scafell Pike but with stunning views. The sun was high by now and warming. The sky was blue and the photography, as was our mood for two allegedly 'grumpy old men', was in the affirmative. We looked out in awe towards Bowfell, the Langdales, across to High Scarth Crag, beyond to Harter Fell and further to the Coniston Fells all rising in the distance. Surely this must be one of the most majestic views in the whole Lake District. The plan was to round on ourselves and return to Wasdale aiming to cross Broad Tongue with Great How to the south on to Maiden Castle cairn before picking up Straighthead Gill down to the car park. Mike knew a different route, or at least he thought he did so we doubled back under Scafell in a northwesterly direction losing height all the time until we arrived now walking not on a path but in bog, which would have been better suited to flippers rather than walking boots, at Groove Gill. Then we crossed a boggier moor down to Fence Wood where we picked up the stone path back to Wasdale. The whole route took 8.21 hours, was 10.65 miles in length and included 4,608 feet of ascent. We arrived back in the National Trust car park hale and hearty still laughing after a great day on the fell, walking and talking.

Surprise Sun

Sunrise a surprise
over crag
with an old lad
mad and a dad
barmy in the moment of their middling age
confronted by one rocky form after another.
Two friends move across the fell laughing at the absurdity.
Like creatures crawling, or foxes dawdling
their movements are captured in the sunlight.
That same light, shines through their memories now.

Figure 19. View over Slight Side

Yorkshire

Today I find myself in my own county sometimes referred to as 'God's own'. The sights, sounds and smells of the Great Yorkshire Show on a sunny day present a montage of sensory experience. We head for the cow sheds. My host, a parishioner, is an expert in animal husbandry and care. We are walking today through mistals, pens and stables heaving with the nation's biggest, best, and most rare beasts. (J. K. Rowling must have taken inspiration in such places.) For my part I feel drawn in and made to feel humble by these farming folk who are putting on their best display in the early morning. The dew is still rising and so is the temperature. A lone piper plays as we cross the threshold wearing member's badges and smiles. 'Waltzing Matilda, I'll come a waltzing Matilda with thee.' A tune played on the chanter, one from my childhood, one both I and my classmates enjoyed singing.

Figure 20. Stephen and Sean at the Great Yorkshire Show

There is no less than an opera or symphony of celebration going on. A classroom of knowledgeable men in white coats and flat caps espying form and linage. This is a stage; the real performers are the animals accompanied by those who have their charge: children in bowler hats, holding boards and sticks are moving pigs around the ring. Farmers turned hairdressers in the shire stables and amongst the sheep sheds addressing their best livestock with scissors and hairdryers. All this poise in a barn, a beautiful one but nevertheless one that reeks of the pastoral: milk, hay and manure combined in a sweet-smelling seductive ah!

Surely this is nativity, men women and children together in celebration showing their best stock to their friends and world. Our Lord Jesus was born among such real and earthed people. Here in any one of these sheds life and faith and hope are born and nurtured. This is where sustainability begins.

At the end of the day having watched the heavy horse class in the main ring and having glugged a jug of Pimm's and Lemonade we returned to the ruminants: Charolais, Short and Long Horns the Jerseys and the Ayrshires all of which were being judged unbeknown to us, allegedly restricting our access. The men too had returned to their women folk with bottles of beer and food and tall tales of the day's work. The scene was pastoral and warm. Heaven was abounding in this place. Just then we were told to leave. 'They're judging,' the security man said! We duly about turned. We were instructed to tell the other security man upon our exit, the man we had walked past into the shed, to do his job properly by the senior security man. We made ourselves scarce and ignored the injunction, but I observed from a distance the boss man publicly humiliate and berate his colleague. I wanted to reach out to them both. I wanted to say, 'You are standing on sacred ground; you are amongst the holy of holies; you are brothers; look at the landscape you are working in; live peaceably.' We walked away but I noted the security man's demeanor following his boss's workout. His shirt was out of his trousers, his stomach was hanging over his belt, he was unshaven and hair unkempt. He looked exhausted, not just worn out by the heat of the day but by the onward march of time and opportunity or not.

The following morning as I completed my dog walk around Broadstone Reservoir Ivy's words came back to me as I reflected on the Great Yorkshire Show a day with a friend which I had hugely enjoyed…

'Walk into yourself Sean…'

Why was this event shaping my morning walk? I found myself weeping huge tears as I crossed the head of the reservoir: weeping for the security man, weeping for his boss, weeping for myself for all the times I have failed to perceive heaven in the midst of the moment, weeping for the fallen and sometimes cruel world we have made and live in, weeping for souls lost in faraway places and sons, daughters, mums and dads returned ceremoniously to church yards. This is not me; I don't feel things in this way.

We all know that humiliation will never yield a good outcome when the demons of the moment prevail. Heaven never forces itself. It appears and we can step into it and be a part of it if we choose to. '*Behold,*' (in other words '*look*') said Jesus, '*I stand at the door and knock.*' [Revelation 3:20]

I can see myself in equal measure in both the boss and the guard. I wanted to reach out to the guard yesterday. I was worried about him. If I could have said how I felt, I would have said something like, 'I don't know your situation but don't let that moment define you or your life. I have never met you, yet I have the capacity to care for you even from this distance. I recognise you are my brother. I will pray for you.' And in praying for this soul, I will also be praying for all those others who are undervalued, mistreated, and dismissed by the supposed powerful of this world.

Another brief encounter with a stranger

Figure 21. Exercise Arduous Serpent, Catterick, North Yorkshire

During the sabbatical I found myself in a forest in Richmond in a challenging military competition hosted by 2nd Medical Brigade. The aim of the competition is to test a variety of military skills over the course of a weekend. Beginning on Friday afternoon and finishing on Sunday afternoon competitors patrol (walk) between each stand at which a military test is executed and marked by the directing staff. It's arduous, and demands survival skills, navigation skills, communication, military knowledge, trust and excellent teamwork. Physical strength, endurance, mental agility, and resilience are tested throughout.

One of the military tests we had to complete late on Saturday afternoon was a medical evacuation of multiple casualties following an explosion. My team completed the stand professionally and competently. In the debrief one of the actors, an ex-soldier, shared with me that he felt a profound anxiety about some parts of operational tours he had completed when he had served in the Army. He was a massive man, not unlike the Great Gable in proportion to most mortals. He was a warrior. He looked frightening with tribal tattoos pinned on rippling muscles and para-military kit adorning his body not dissimilar to one of the powerful heavy Shire horses in the show ring. We talked only for a short while and then I hugged him, that was all I could do. I held him as I might my own son in an embrace for a moment and said, 'It's all right. Thank you for your service. I'm sorry. Let 'it' (the trauma) all go.' I walked silently on to the next stand with my team.

In moments such as these we can occasionally catch a glimpse of ourselves an insight into our own vulnerabilities and our strengths. The path we take in our own lives perhaps enables us to deliver a particular response into the present. I hope my responses are understanding and compassionate. Christ came into the world as the light of all people [John 1:9] and whose example those who serve him are commissioned to follow.

I remember once a long time ago when my then young wife received some bad news. I was standing at the end of the hospital cot in bewilderment as the Doctor walked away looking at my wife's tears of disappointment and her hope ebbing away. I was trying to think of something profoundly theological to say whilst the woman, a stranger in the next bed, came and sat at the side of my wife and quietly hugged her. I have never felt as inadequate as a human being in my entire life. Sometimes all anyone can do is hold someone physically in their arms. Just maybe that is enough. Is that the prayer, the joining of humanity and compassion?

Another moment of compassionate reflection was watching an aged man being helped up from the communion rail in his church by his male partner. Oh, there had been rumours as there always were in those days, but he gave money and time and so the naysayers kept their guard. I cannot ever remember being so completely overwhelmed by this act of love, a man lifting up his much cherished and loved aging partner. It was a complete disclosure of their relationship to me and one of the most heroic and courageous actions I have ever witnessed.

In this poem I try to capture some of the moments of reflection from my living, through the lens of theology and scripture and from my sabbatical walking.

Moments

Gone now the moments when you were in your prime
running the gauntlet, testing your ambitions against the young.
Rather dragged now into life face to face with reality
and with a determined hopefulness.
Abandonment of preconceptions ...
Acknowledgement of the situation ...
resurrect the fabric of faith.

No one is perfect, not one – rather we exist as shards of a whole held
together by the delicate moments when the heavens bequeath love.
Accepting such a gift in public reminds me,
'Death is naked before God'.
There is no hiding.

I am stripped almost bare, with black witch-like toes from walking.
I can choose how to walk on into the next haunting.
Broken and wrecked on the mountainside where the testament of faith was
handed to my ancestors... can I do justice and receive mercy?
'You shall have no other gods before me.'

This is not alchemy.
This is faith, and life and truth.
In His light I will arise,
and I will come again this way.
I will come walking differently
with feet rested, washed and pink,
with compassion and
... with love.

'Walk into yourself Sean...'

Beauty

A Wikipedia internet dictionary search of the word beauty resulted in:

'What is beauty in a human? Beauty is a combination of qualities such as form, proportion, and colour in a human face (or other object) that delights the sight. These last words are important: Beauty does not exist itself; it exists in the eye of the beholder.'

Ralph Waldo Emerson the great American philosopher and abolitionist of the nineteenth century is quoted as saying; *'Though we travel the world over to find the beautiful, we must carry it with us, or we find it not.'* Emerson's *ESSAY XII Art*

'I have been touched by beauty; I am blessed to have been chosen by her.'
Sean Robertshaw

The new perspective that comes with slowing down and walking is truly fascinating. Human beings have evolved in such a way that they are designed to be constantly moving through their landscape. Those people that move all the time in these days are not best adapted for modern society which is, for many people, working in front of a computer screen for hours on end. One of the great gifts of being human is the ability to perform quite complex tasks whilst on the move. Our ancestors were hunter gatherers. They moved through the landscape watching, waiting, then running quite literally after their daily bread. Is it any surprise that people today especially men like to play video games which simulate hunting, fighting, and surviving. There is perhaps a Walter Mitty hiding somewhere inside of us all whereby we all seek to be heroic in our deepest fantasies.

As I moved through the landscape, all heroic thoughts now behind me, I began to notice the detail. By shifting focus, I began to notice the miniature world of nature beneath my feet: bluebells, sorrel, fern, buttercup, lupine, daisy, lichens, mountain ash, oak, 'the whole of nature mine' springing up from the ground, and in a vast array of colours. Poppies velvet and red, cornflowers violet, roses crawling through hedgerows pink, thistles purple and bold. Life crawling out of a bog. It is beautiful down there. It is all coming up from the bottom.

Figure 22. Cotton Grass growing out of a fell side pool near Silver Howe

Ground

Below the eye-line,
below the usual dull carriage of blankness
lies a mystery, it is unnoticed!
Hiding every day on the ground floor.
Life grows silently out of the dust and reaches up into the day.
When the sun shines
and the ground is wet with the dew of the morning
pollinated plants crawled on by ants and
buzzed on by bees, and all those things that bite and sting
bring blooms which appear and disappear
year in and year on.
Marvel at the sight rising out of the ground,
nature sings brightly through the summer light.

As a regular visitor to the Lakes, I have crossed Coniston Water several times to visit Brantwood, once the home of the Victorian writer John Ruskin, now owned by the Brantwood Trust. Ruskin wrote on a variety of topics: botany, art, travel, and politics to name but a few. I can understand why. His mind must have been extended in the Lakeland landscape. It is one which invites the beholder into it. No one thing is beautiful in this landscape the whole of it is one of awe-inspiring splendour as it rotates through each season.

Figure 23. Early Purple Orchid surrounded by Bog Asphodel

The view from Brantwood across the lake into the Southern Fells is breathtaking. The fell rises as a wall in front of you 2,633 feet to the summit of Coniston Old Man flanked by Brim Fell to the left and Wetherlam to the right. These mighty mountains are silent stones. Nowadays they gaze down upon the activities of men and women as they paddle along the shorelines of the lake finding enjoyment, friendship, and community in the valley bottom.

But it has not always been so. The steep ascent directly from Coniston village following Church Beck past Miners Bridge reveals the workings of a now redundant copper mine which was at its busiest during the 1800s supporting many families and increasing the size of the local population. Heritage funding in 2016 transformed the visitor experience at these mines. The project focused on conservation; these mountains that once bled their copper into the local and national economy now open their treasurers for the many inquisitive visitors and tourists. I'm sure Ruskin would have approved of their repurposing.

'Never lose an opportunity of seeing anything beautiful, for beauty is God's handwriting.' Attributed to John Ruskin.

Mountaineer

My niece is only small, but she is mighty. This is a standing family joke and one we all enjoy as a term of endearment given over to 'The mighty Anna'. Although small, not inappropriately so, she is something of a perfectionist which can be both irritating when parking the car and engaging when seeking to understand something about the fells.

She is a first-class navigator and as a walking companion something of an expert on the Lakeland Fells, knowing each one with an encyclopedic level of knowledge. She has walked them all, at least once. Two hundred and fourteen Wainwright peaks bagged and collected!

Anna joined me with Will my son for a week in Borrowdale. I joyfully abandoned Stuart Marshall who wrote the equivalent of a Royal Marine guide to bagging the Wainwright's and resorted unashamedly to her sense of utility: the greatest number of peaks for least effort. Other than insisting that we walked the western mountain slopes of Buttermere incorporating Red Pike, High Stile, High Crag, Haystacks and Fleetwith Pike all above 2,000 feet (other than Haystacks which sits just below at 1,959 feet) on one day, I made no other demands. It was 'bag as many peaks as possible' week.

The days panned out well, two peaks in Watendlath on Monday which provided a rally style drive along a rising, narrowing single track road. When we arrived in the National Trust car park, we bagged Grange Fell and Great Crag before retiring to the tearoom for a 'cuppa'.

The following day, Tuesday, we parked at the scenic Ashness Bridge and covered the three peaks overlooking Keswick and Thirlmere: Walla Crag, Bleaberry Fell and High Seat, a walk that was mostly wet underfoot and attracted irritable clouds that didn't know quite how to behave.

Wednesday was something of a hotchpotch setting off early in the car in variable but windy conditions to bag some outlying Wainwrights.

The first peak, Little Mell Fell, straight up to the top, quick hug in the wind and directly back down into the car. Then we crossed the valley to Great Mell Fell, a trickier ascent in by now humid conditions which sapped our mood as much as our legs. Then Gowbarrow Fell. Once at the top of these peaks lurking on the very edge of the eastern Lake District, we enjoyed views of Skiddaw and Blencathra, and over the flat plains to the northeast. There were occasional glimpses of Ullswater in the south and in the far distance to the north the Solway Firth in Scotland. It was worth the work out. We now headed to St John's in the Vale. Leaving my fellow travellers in the car park to perambulate the quaint church dedicated to St John, I bolted up High Rigg above the church for views down Thirlmere and over to Raven Crag lookout. I was really racing by now, enjoying this period of sabbatical and an increasing level of fitness and motivation.

Pulling out of the car park in Vale we aimed ourselves north past Bassenthwaite Lake and across to Binsey. By now the weather had closed in. Visibility was reduced to 25 metres. I powered up the 1,467 feet. At the top I snapped a picture and ran back down to the car. Five Wainwrights bagged. The physical effort of the day left me feeling euphoric and determined. My fitness, resilience and all-round health were improving. I was cheered on by my son and niece. Each night we returned to the Borrowdale youth hostel to cook, play table tennis, talk, and sleep. That night, I needed sleep.

Having left Borrowdale hostel on the Thursday morning we drove to and squeezed the car into the last space in the National Trust car park in Buttermere. We, that is Anna, Will and I, absorbed sun cream and insect repellent into our skin, found caps, grabbed our day sacks, and walked around the disarming and charming northern end of Buttermere, mixing with the tourists before beginning battle.

The path up Red Pike is direct. Straight up from bottom to top 2,476 feet. Up through the forest to the end of the tree line, then over the stile and from there zigzagging on the switchbacks up the fell, picking up the fall of Sour Milk Gill before arriving for a quick refuel of tiffin at Bleaberry Tarn. The summit from here lies approximately another towering 836 feet above. It's a brutal scramble onto the top.

It was hard going and her 'mightiness' was sure she wanted us to press on leaving her behind until she arrived in her own time which we did. I took a picture of the arrival which did not go down well. However, for posterity the moment was caught and cast forever in its ether frame. The rest of the ridge was uneventful other than Anna was able to describe in great detail the surrounding fells, heights, distances, best places to park and walk from and to and she also pointed out some of the challenges of walking in Ennerdale, a part of the Lakes I had yet to explore. Pre-warned and pre-armed, I was thankful.

There was a most charming raven who stayed close to us throughout much of this part of the walk, calling out from the air, occasionally dropping onto the mountain path, and performing aerial acrobatics such as inverse flying without seeming to somewhat ironically ruffle a feather. Eat your heart out Tom Cruise! It was quite a show which we rewarded with our sandwich crusts and apple cores. The raven was a comedic and competent performer and unusually sociable.

Raven

The darkness sparkles bright in your intelligent eye.
Scrutiny, curiosity a levelled watching
as you spin round and over in the sky.
The breeze whips at the thinning air
and you fly and fall.
A bolting black jet, races, and dives.
Acrobat, suddenly halted you stoop
flash your wing
watch again and bow.
The show goes on with you.

As we moved across Comb Crag and White Cove towards Gamlin End my companions were weary and indolent, far less inclined than I to face Haystacks. We negotiated a plan, and I went forward with vigour almost throwing myself down the mountainside to Scarth Gap, before running back up Haystacks. The whole movement was invigorating. I could feel my breath heavy but steady as I climbed back up to the top of Haystacks. I took a picture of Innominate Tarn, (meaning without a name) where I briefly paused to pay homage to the great and late Alfred Wainwright in whose steps I was following. Wainwright described the tarn as: *'Haystacks' finest jewel…a small shallow sheet of water in which flourishes the lovely bogbean and over which Great Gable and Pillar stand guard in ceaseless watch. A lonely spot of haunting charm…life seems good here. It is a venue for happy pilgrimages.'* [www.alfredwainwright.co.uk/wainwright-pilgrimage]

Alfred Wainwright died on January 20, 1991. It was in this place he requested that his ashes should be scattered. I did not tarry long, but long enough to catch the moment and to reflect that I would, God willing, come back to this spot again. Most likely at a time when I would not be able to run but more probably hobble humbly to the place with no name that I might join with the many million names that are written in the book of life. I was humbled by the vista; gratitude and exhilaration were my two overarching feelings. On the fells you see the oddest things. On that day was a push chair and two parents sharing a picnic with their child, wilderness, or picnic site? Who knows, but it was a surreal moment.

Setting off downward at a similar pace to the upward ascent skipping past those I had met on the way up my aim was to get to Scarth Gap and pick up my two fellow walkers. We arrived at the same time and headed off northwards across Buttermere Fell back to the head of the lake for refreshments. The walking was hot, and progress was quiet and ponderous. Time seemed to slow down as we walked shrouded in our own cocoons for a few miles.

Arriving at the Bridge Hotel we flopped into the shaded outdoor seating, ordered cold drinks and food then sat in the last of the afternoon's hot sun, boots and socks off, soon guzzling burgers and chips, aggrandized by various sauces. Delicious!

This, however, was not the end of our walking. There were weighty bags packed and ready to go in the car boot. We were heading up to Honister youth hostel where we intended to leave the car overnight. There was a renewed air of excitement in our little party as we climbed up and over the slate mine route which carried us high above the valley floor and road below. Will led out, Anna and I taking a more leisurely pace, our frames not as vast as the powerful second row forward striding out effortlessly before us.

It took us well over an hour with all our equipment to get to the top of Fleetwith Pike but the views made it so worthwhile. We 'ummed and ahed' about where to pitch our tents but opted ultimately despite the strong chilling wind to stay on the top. The idea was to photograph the night sky. Anna wanted to take a compositional photograph of the Solar System over Great Gable: ambitious, yes, but this is mightiness at work. Despite the chilling wind we three mystics erected the tents, all three of them, and then watched the dawdling sunset recede almost at the speed of our earlier afternoon perambulation. The sun gone, so was the heat.

Figure 24. View from Fleetwith Pike over Buttermere and Crumock Water

Sundown, and now we had time to wait for the correct moment to take the picture. The earliest opportunity was 2220 hours. It passed with not enough darkness and too many clouds. So sometime after 2300 hours there was another chance but again now lashing rain, wind, cloud cover and just being very cold in our summer sleeping bags defeated our effort.

Little stirring was noted. At 0610 hours the rain abated just in time to avoid a flood in my tent. Upon her mightiness's command, 'ANYONE AWAKE' we arose from hibernation shivering, felled our wringing camp, retraced our steps back to the car, piled our kit and selves into the vehicle, turbo-charged the heating and headed off to what was referenced as 'Spoons' (aka Wetherspoons) in Keswick for breakfast. The second row again led the charge!

I fancied a coffee and was desperately trying not to commit the deadly sin of gluttony meaning, like any good parent, I reluctantly declined the Full-English, but I was enamoured by the coffee machine which ministered to my every need each time I pushed the button marked latte.

Warmed by milk, bacon, hash browns and coffee and or civilization we headed off to Tarn Hows to complete Black Fell, not high level, more of a jewel nestled in the Southern Fells.

Upon arrival I ascended from the National Trust car park alone and at a gait. My nearly three months of walking had by now gifted me with speed. I was glad of my own company and quickly covered the miles using the walking poles skillfully. I roughly calculated that the poles allowed me to considerably extend every one in three downward steps. I was back almost before I had gone whilst my companions dozed in the car, enjoyed the warm sun, and watched the rainbows magically appear and dissolve, like 'Snow'.[5]

Fluid Movement

Running with poles became fun. The movement was fluid and natural not unlike in my mind's-eye a pack of hounds hunting, which is one of the most beautiful sights on earth.

Anyone who has ever seen a foxhound or beagle in full cry leading a pack of hounds across the moorland, under gates and fences, over walls and across bridleways and water courses will know what I mean.

---

[5] See page 4

The movement of hounds is thrilling like a viscous liquid finding its own course. Hunting is a much-misunderstood visceral blood sport in the country.

My late and noble friend Nigel Hinchliffe Esquire would know exactly what I mean about the hounds. A man of mirth, equally edgy, engaging, bright and funny, a wheeler dealer and fixer, a local character in my town. Writer, actor, and newsagent. Nigel was a man-mountain and former president of the Pennine Foxhounds.

He enjoyed welcoming singers from Derbyshire, North Yorkshire, Cumbria and Northumbria to The Fleece Inn in Holme village for a meeting at which singing and shared friendship was celebrated.

The old ways still have power. The stories are there to dwell on and retell. They bind communities and as the night gets older the tales get taller. 'John Peel' is a well-known song from the hunter's repertoire which recalls the huntsman calling to the hounds and the whipper-inners.

> Did ye ken John Peel wid his cwote sae grey?
> Did ye ken John Peel at the breck o' day?
> Did ye ken John Peel gayin' far, far away -
> Wie his hoons and his horn in a mwornin'?
>
> Chorus:
>
> For the sound o' the horn caw'd me fra my bed.
> As the cry o' the hoons he often led,
> For Peel's view holla wad waken the dead,
> Or a fox frae his lair in a mwornin.'

My walking began to flow. I learned to navigate with greater skill, and as I gained the ability to hold the bigger landscape in my mind within the walk, my mind became free and began to move more fluidly too. I began to trust my instincts and my new learning as I moved across and over the mountains through the passes. I quickly guzzled up the miles and felt euphoric at the end of the chase, happier in my mind and fuller in my heart. I do not wonder Brother Francis turned his back on a merchant's life to live simply in the landscape he has become associated with. The Umbrian hills and plains are beautiful, majestic places also.

These wilderness pastures are a rich source of food for one's soul and the tarns and pools presented moments of unabashed nakedness and cooling. Yes, '*The Lord is my Shepherd I shall not want.*'
[Psalm 23 verses 1 NIV]

Figure 25. Nigel Hinchliffe Esq. painted by Trevor Stubbly RP. *Nigel in Chinatown Manchester* – this picture appeared at Nigel's funeral, so I snapped it on my phone. It appears here with permission

Figure 26. Will, Anna and Sean pictured above Derwent Water

Mountaineer Continued

Black Crag, and another Wainwright bagged, with beautiful views down Lake Windermere with a striking trig point and separate cairn. The day was now done for me. We retreated to level climbs and flowing conversation at Coniston Water, parking briefly in the village to buy authentic Cumberland sausage from the butcher, which was immediately placed in our cold bag. We then lay in the hot sun on the pebbles of the northern shore and watched the people there on that day on that piece of earth and how they dwelled therein. People-watching. The laziness of the day was welcome after a poor night's sleep. Eventually sloth gave way to activity. Reluctantly we left the lakeside and headed back to Yorkshire and home, Borrowdale and 'mightiness' indelibly etched on our hearts and family memories to share and tell in the future. Mighty Anna, mountaineer and our companion had conquered again and had led us joyfully across the mountain tops, mostly with a smile and always with confidence.

Troutbeck Revisited

I found myself walking in Troutbeck on the hottest day ever on record in the United Kingdom. I remained as I usually do, on task. After all I was there to walk, an uplift of a few degrees in the heat index was not going to change my plan which was to walk the heights surrounding Troutbeck. Luckily, I had secured nearby accommodation from a friend. It was on my mind that this was a well-known area for Wordsworth and his sister Dorothy. I was keen not to waste the opportunity to walk in this distinct area of the Lakes.

I'd planned to walk five peaks, two on the eastern flank, then Troutbeck Tongue, followed by the westerly slopes of the valley. I was on the fell at 0800. Walking has become my habit and not walking causes me to feel peculiar. I was soon up some 1,568 feet to the summit of Sour Howes where there was a gentle breeze, but the heat was noticeably up and increasing. It reminded me of the Iraq desert and a good friend from that part of my life to whom I sent a text. He responded instantly with equal enthusiasm. Despite the years of relative silence, the bond still existed! Having gained height quickly I flashed across the fell to Sallows for a beautiful view out over Windermere before descending northwards and then wending my way across the fell to the trailhead for the walk into the back of Troutbeck to return via The Tongue. I was hot and had drunk a good deal of my 3 litres of water. Having taken the longer hike to the back of the Tongue I had walked very slowly up the hillside catching the thin hot air, Turning south I continued to the peak where I grabbed a quick bite, cheese and salami sandwiches melting nicely into the wholemeal bread, delicious! It was getting much hotter, and I was re-evaluating my walk and plan. Two more peaks felt physically out of reach. The sun was absorbing every ounce of my energy. I needed to stop and rehydrate, re-apply sunscreen, and think about the best way to return safely to my billet.

I disliked having to admit to myself that my plan needed reviewing, but this trend was becoming more familiar and I more accepting of the need adapt to the situation in front of me. I was fading faster than I had anticipated and the baking heat would not relent. It continued to intensify, meaning I was putting myself in unnecessary danger. Therefore, I took the fastest descent directly down from the cairn marking the summit of the Tongue and shaded under a friendly Mountain Ash on the bridge crossing Troutbeck. Here I drank the last of my water and replenished it from the inviting cool beck. Having now checked myself over and engaged with the map and compass I was ready to walk again. It was still hot, almost too hot, which caused me to ponder briefly getting in the water to cool down as I had in Easedale Tarn on a previous hike out across Grassmere Common to High Raise. What determined the outcome was an almost empty tube of sunscreen, meaning I would have washed off any residual protection if I had gone into the water. Decision made. I walked the three kilometers directly back to the campsite.

The westerly peaks were out of mind at that point, but in sight all the way back, waiting for another day. It took me less than an hour to walk back. When I arrived, I was shattered and overheated. It would have been challenging to walk any further safely that day. I jumped in the shower, cooled down, slept for an hour then ate another sandwich. I have lived to tell the tale: 9.63 miles, 4 hours 21 minutes, 2,983 feet of elevation, stupidly covered off on the hottest day on record in the United Kingdom, one on which I drank just over 4 litres of water. But importantly three Wainwright peaks bagged. I am still on task! I ponder what is becoming of my church congregants in this heat.

Return

My favourite Christmas story appears only in Matthew's Gospel chapter 2 verses 1-12. It is the visit of the Magi to the baby Jesus and the Holy Family. It is not an easy journey. We hear that the Magi are guided by a star which appeared in the skies to the east, most likely in Persia. It eventually guides them to Bethlehem and indeed to the newly born infant. They come to pay homage to Jesus. After presenting their gifts they are warned by an angel in a dream not to return to Herod the regional king, whom they had mistakenly visited earlier. The reader is informed, 'They returned home by a different route.'

A cautious friend of mine often comments, 'We can always go back.' A psychotherapist in my congregation once leaned over and said into my ear rather mischievously, 'There is no going back.' But my mind is drifting, I am beginning to think about what is happening for the people at home and in my parishes, and how they are all getting along.

Once whilst driving to Danby Forest mountain-bike park in North Yorkshire with a highly motivated CEO I missed our turn off the main road. Having missed the turn the Satnav indicated we needed to make a U-turn. My companion wanted to continue along the road we were on. 'We'll eventually get there,' he said. I pulled the car over to check. The journey was estimated to be 20 minutes longer if we did not make the U-turn, which I immediately completed to 'get us back on track'.

I wonder how good I am at making U-turns. Or will I because of this sabbatical become more willing to do them? Maybe there are other turns I need to make and reflect upon before returning to work. That space, the one I made in the garden, is beginning to show signs of new growth, but I feel there is still some weeding to be done in some of the new borders.

Is it a time to go back? 'A time to keep and a time to throw away' [Ecclesiastes 3:6b]. These day's I am less sure about U-turns.

The professor of chemistry with whom I walked out of the Langdale valley in a westerly direction suggests that circular walks are false and are less satisfying than walking a linear route to somewhere for a particular purpose. I had not considered this suggestion in any depth whilst planning my routes around the Lake District mountain tops. To get back to my car or accommodation I would usually walk in a circle, or occasionally catch a bus from a finishing point. But of course, this makes sense in the light of my companion's comment.

My present walk is mostly secular. I have found that I am distancing myself from the last 25 years plus of working and as much of Christendom as I am able. Am I walking away from rather than into? Not away from Christ or faith, reading scripture, prayer, worship, or any of those things. Rather I am walking away from something which feels fractured in me and the world I usually inhabit. I am not ungrateful. The life I have lived, certainly as an adult, has been within the wider Christian family. This life, my life as soldier and servant, has provided me and my family with a home and stability. It has given us degrees of opportunity and lines of support. We have been loved and cared for. Yet to feel whole I need to move on in some way: emotionally, morally, or perhaps even physically? I realize a desire within to move away from those things that are not good for me, those things that eat up the energy and life that I am discovering and enjoying through the walking. Walking in circles is one thing; it may appear safer to know where you aim at least to return to? Walking in straight lines from one place to a future destination appears to suggest purpose? Is this a difference between walking and pilgrimage?

The beginning of this sabbatical was planned with almost military precision. I knew which days I would walk, what I would eat, carry and so on; yet the day I set off I had not planned for feeling so lonely or alone. Neither had I really tested my body properly and whilst I could have carried on, I discovered very soon that my load was too heavy. I could not continue carrying it for three months. Neither was I in control of the weather, and my mood had been dark for too long. I had forgotten the freedom of the high peaks; rather I had experienced solitude in the valley bottom and daily grind of work. Desolation was around me. Had I created this situation, or did it just come to be over time? It was not just in that moment that I felt like this. It was the complete realization of where I had arrived at this point in my life. One learns fast on the fell-side. I quickly reassessed and restructured my sabbatical time into the art of the possible and importantly the pragmatic and mostly enjoyable. Enjoyable is the one piece of life I soon began to rediscover, my purpose and being, family and true friends. Continually striving and carrying responsibility leaves its indelible mark on one. Leading, caring, monitoring, remembering, forgoing that deeper experience enjoyment and fulfillment can soon lead one down false trails and pathways. If you are unhappy in your environment, then it is not rocket-science to assess how one needs to change it or your approach to it.

I needed to return home ... I literally did at the end of the first day. [Luke15:18 NIV] *'I will set out and go back to my father and say to him: Father, I have sinned against heaven and against you.'*

I needed to return to the root of my being ... after finding out I was not nearly as able as I had anticipated I would be. [Exodus 20:2a NIV] *'I am the LORD your God, who brought you out of Egypt, out of the land of slavery.'*

I needed to return to the source of faith ...which somehow seemed located on the mountain slopes out in the world. [John14:6 NIV] *'Jesus answered, "I am the way and the truth and the life. No one comes to the Father except through me."*

And: I needed to be a happier more content version of myself. [Mark 10:49b NIV] *'Jesus stopped and said, "Call him." So they called to the blind man, "Cheer up! On your feet! He's calling you."*

Is this what Ivy was asking me about? Is this what happens when one walks into oneself? Did I need to do a U-turn, go backwards, or commit to both? The civil rights activist and writer, Maya Angelou wrote in: *I Know Why the Caged Bird Sings*, '*You can't really know where you are going until you know where you have been.*'

That first day walking began with a sense of false optimism as I went up onto the mountain top; I must have been mistaken or deluded or both.

Walkers coming down the mountain said, 'You must be mad going up there. You'll kill yourself.' How arrogant I was, and how small I had made God in my mind! When the rains came down, and the wind howled, and I was literally blinded left without the ability to use my reading glasses and map I was lost.

Suddenly I was a lamb and in need of a mighty God to save me. I knew I was on top of the mountain. I even knew which mountain top, and I was confident that I would not die. I had all I needed on my back, but it was no help to me because I did not have the will to use it. Spiritually I was as good as dead. What had flowed out over the years was less than had flowed in, I was running on empty.

Every fibre of my being hurt. I was wrecked as the storm raged around me. I allowed all those hurts and feelings from the past to come to the surface. Yes, a kind of madness had set in. Would walking resolve it? When eventually the cloud broke for a single moment, I realized I had walked in blissful ignorance over Cofa Pike and had picked up Deepdale Hause. I was descending into Patterdale although I was many miles off my route, in fact walking in completely the wrong direction, but now I was rejoicing. I was still alive. I had survived the storm. I called my wife. I wanted to hear her voice.

Me: 'Hello. I'm okay. Can you look at what time the bus leaves Glenridding?'

Sally: 'Just after 6pm.'

Me: 'Thank you.'

I started running to get to the bus stop. The next bus was at 8pm. My life would have to be different now.

That could never happen again. It was a long journey back to where my car was parked.[6]

Wind

Abruptly the swell up storm is banging on the flap of my rucksack.
Why this thundering below?
This is an unusual altitude.
Travelling at speed exceeding my expectations
suddenly I am shot through, broken, and falling down to earth.
I didn't hear the bang, but someone had taken a shot
or was that my body hitting the headstone?
Flat and beaten I lie in the cloud, heart racing bleeding out.
I try to practise breathing
and wait for a break in the storm to regroup.
Finding the map, I point my compass.
It has not pointed this way for some time.
Returning down from this lofty mountain place
I will come again by a different route.

Barbara Brown Taylor in her book *Leaving Church,* HarperOne, (2012) makes this point:

> *'By now I expected to be a seasoned parish minister wearing black clergy shirts grown grey from frequent washing. I expected to love children who hung on my legs after Sunday morning services until they grew up and had children of their own. I expected to spend the rest of my life writing sermons, leading worship, delivering pastoral care to the living, and burying the dead – not for 20 years but for all my years. I even expected to be buried in the same red vestments in which I was ordained.'*

---

[6] See page 6.

During this last three months I have engaged differently with the living out of faith. It is has not stopped me being kind, paying my tithe, or worshipping God but it has caused me to ignore the 800 emails or so that are currently sitting in an inbox somewhere craving my attention and best thinking. I have not stopped loving my family nor my church family; in fact, I seem to have had more time to attend to their specific needs and to think about them.

I have not ceased to pray for or reach out to those with need, nor have I stopped celebrating the great joys of marriage, friendship, and love. Neither have I stopped writing. I have written about life and faith differently. Not on Saturday for a Sunday sermon with a text to follow but deliberately when the Spirit has moved me. I have been blessed by not having to think big Church or excessively consider world events.

This walking into oneself is now becoming a greater challenge. I am realising that I am not intended to walk in circles. I think Reverend Bob Jackson the church growth expert said something along the lines of the Church not being a roundabout, rather a purposeful Gospel train that moves people along and builds a new community. Am I learning that the true pilgrim walks without too much certainty but confidently with a sense of promise? As I behold the prospect of putting on the old clothes in a week or two's time, I am not feeling thrilled about the task ahead. I am done with dogma, schemes, and programs. I want to be alive to new possibility, challenge, and change. Bruce Springsteen sings, '*Big wheels roll through fields where sunlight streams. Meet me in the land of hope and dreams.*' I wonder, who will I meet if I can make it there?

Bad News

Towards the end of the sabbatical period, I was on the high street in Keswick. I left my car parked on the vicar's drive. He happens to be a longtime friend and colleague. The Keswick Convention which has been hosted since 1875 by Christians in that place was happening in town. My friend was happily chatting about the nuancing of the conference. This clause, that belief, why someone does not appear on the conference book list etc... He was in there alive, vital, happy, and engaged. As soon as he started talking 'Church' I started running for the hills. I literally looked up at Cat Bells and wondered how long it would take me to get to the top? My son who was with me without prompt later noted that he had watched me glaze over! The usual 'church talk' was not in any way attractive to me, it was almost redundant, removed from my vocabulary. I remember it felt like an unwelcome memory. It didn't belong to me. Anyway, back to the Keswick high street.

Whilst walking past a public house window there was a notice that read something like: (my paraphrase) '*If you are in a same sex relationship, or you are gender neutral, live with a disability, don't eat meat or do, or suffer with mental health issues, or if you are a person of colour, a refugee or dislocated from your own country... then you are safe here with us.*' I stopped and rejoiced in the messaging from this business. I wanted to join this ekklesia. I naturally embraced this subversive vibe. It was speaking to my new sabbatical self. It was with some mirth that I wondered how many of the Convention participants had entered these premises and if so, how safe they felt there? Neither did I enter.

... thinking Church: I miss something of your familiarity, but there are conversations I am not missing.

Rain

Hail rain, ordained in rising cloud
wet upon the face, a trace, something new
like tears made for joy bursting through
elemental energy pulls the mountains into view.

The crafter cut these shapes in granite.
Stretching away pylon lines sizzling in the rain crossing the blue.

Tufts blow and ewes bleat for their lambs
tucked away sheltering under mangers full of hay.

Whispering in the wet the Holy Ghost moves
the fell a sponge of glue that holds,
firmament flowing over summit.
Rain down, rain town, rain falling-down.

Dogs

I have only managed a few walks with my dog Scout in the Lakes. He is 11 years old now and although fit and happy to go for local dog walks and swims, 15 miles over crag and rock might interrupt the sleep he seems to enjoy these days. Scout has been our family dog since he was 9 weeks old. He is a Labrador Retriever once trained to the field trial standard. He occasionally remembers this fact if I ever blow a whistle at him which I tend not to do these days. I have too much respect for him. Scout reads us well. We rarely tell him anything. He tells us when we are late to walk or feed him or if anyone is around who he is not sure ought to be.

Whilst walking on Haystacks Alfred Wainwright's favourite Lakeland fell near Buttermere I bumped into a man with a dog. It was a beautiful Hungarian Wire Haired Vizsla, a hardy athletic medium-sized dog. Even though I was essentially running I stopped to share a word with the man and admire the dog which was on a short lead. Whilst returning from the summit of the mountain the man still ascending with the said dog on a lead had got himself into a bit of a mess and had lost confidence. I suggested he let the dog off the lead if it would stay with him as he was literally carrying this creature up the last bit of the mountain which was proving dangerous for them both. He could not, or he did not trust the dog off the lead, nor his own ability to climb with it on the lead. 'Can I come down with you?' he asked me, shaken. I pointed out that I was running and that he had the ability to set both himself and the dog free. I went for help and signed his partner 25 metres further down the mountain back up to him.

Are we that which we make ourselves to be? A beautiful fit dog tethered by a mixture of love and fear. A man willing to risk his life rather than let go of the lead which attached him to the dog. A wife 25 metres away ignoring her husband whilst remembering her last ascent of this fell as a child with her father, 'before he died' she said.

This scene reminded me of the popular 2009 US film *Up* which centres on an elderly widower Carl and a Wilderness Explorer, who go on a journey to fulfil a promise that Carl made to his late wife Ellie. It is a film about getting old, about regret and about realizing that life is messy and out of control, as much as you might try to make it otherwise. But it is also a film about love, compassion and making sure that every day counts.

I kept running down, running away from the chaos, running away from absurdity maybe running away from normal life. Running. I did a lot of that during the Covid pandemic. Why am I running all the time? Have I been running all my life? Do I think running makes me immortal? What am I afraid of?

Scout and I stopped in a field this morning. As I sat on the dewy grass he came and sat at the side of me and pressed his head into mine. I knotted and threw his lead, one I merely carry as a prop to signal to other dog walkers that I am kindred to them. I threw it as far as I could from a sitting position. Scout keenly watched it fall, looked at me and waited for the words of command, 'Go out,' and he was off. Our favourite game began again, and the years rolled away for us both as we played out our well-rehearsed game on the Yorkshire heath in the sunshine covered in birdsong, both set free for a moment and happy. 'Go out!' I will need to keep doing that if I am going to live differently.

Taigh Mor (translation: 'The Mansion')

Matthew 11:28-39 'Come to me, all you who are weary and burdened, and I will give you rest. Take my yoke upon you and learn from me, for I am gentle and humble in heart, and you will find rest for your souls. For my yoke is easy and my burden is light.'

There was a brief but important moment which took place four weeks into this sabbatical, a moment when I turned towards the south and headed into North Wales. I had been invited to a well-being retreat hosted by the Taigh Mor Foundation. The retreat took place over three days on a beautiful estate on the banks of the river Dee. Our expert professor Andy McCann based his philosophy on sound research, his own and others, and the proven techniques which support our natural circadian rhythm. That is the physical, mental, and behavioural changes that follow a 24-hour cycle. Such natural processes respond primarily to light and dark and affect most living things, including human beings. I had no idea what to expect. There was a short read into the course, just a few pages which told me more about our accommodation than anything else. The staff, hosting, accommodation, and catering were truly excellent which made the learning experience a relaxing positive one.

I arrived to be greeted by a small gathering of people most of whom I had not met previously. We shared a buffet-style finger lunch and gingerly began that round of introductions where you try to remember names, but all too soon forget them again. Introductions and food over the first session commenced. Participants were asked to consider their overall health, well-being and fitness and what improvements we might choose to make.

Without going into every detail here, what was most striking was the content which was based on the issues we each face in daily life and robust scientific research which addresses some of them. Over those few days our parasympathetic nervous system and brain became the focus of our own attention. We were encouraged to employ and practise different lifestyle techniques as we assimilated the course.

Breathing, eating, exercise, sleep, and being generous were the main topics that we explored and considered. Our mentors stimulated each of us to assess and practise the exercises that were offered to us as they walked us through their own experiences. We quickly gelled as a group, each of us soon immersed in the course. The content made good sense, was accessible and offered opportunities to consider what simple changes if any participants may choose to make to their lifestyle to positively affect their well-being.

One of the sessions focused on breathing. These techniques were particularly insightful for me. 'Take control of your breathing' is a mantra ingrained in me from training in the Army. How we breathe enables much in our bodies. Any elite athlete first gains mastery over their breathing. We were each given a paper straw and encouraged to breathe through it for two minutes. It was a challenge, especially when adding a simple exercise such as walking across a lawn. Using the straw makes it challenging to expel the toxic build-up of CO_2. The brain screams at the lungs to exhale the build-up of carbon dioxide as fast as possible. I discovered that simple breathing exercises, when combined with mindful practices can make a difference to how one approaches the situations, people, or the day one may find oneself in.

Walking mindfully and breathing purposefully have aided my attempts to become contented. The old anxieties seem to have a weaker grip on my mind when I breathe well.

Maintaining improved control of one's breathing can be a significant game changer when going into a stressful situation. Resting, recuperation, eating well are simple lifestyle choices to develop to improve one's overall well-being.

One of the most fascinating topics during the presentations was being compassionate. Research indicates that being of a caring disposition improves one's overall health, mainly by giving the carer a sense of purpose and meaning. Christians are encouraged to be both compassionate and generous in their living. This idea is nurtured in the scriptures. At the offertory in the main service of Holy Communion, also known as the celebration of the Eucharist (Greek: thanksgiving) Christians hear of the injunction to 'love one's neighbour' whilst simultaneously affirming that all we have comes from God, both material and moral. Many of our readings concerning the early Church show the emergent followers of Jesus as being characterised by their demonstrations of love for one another in their sharing of possessions e.g., Acts 4:32-35. Generosity is a constant theme in the major world religions, so perhaps we should not be surprised that it contributes to human health and well-being. Generosity flows from the Creator because God is merciful, benevolent, and generous.

Oxytocin is a chemical produced in the brain. It is a neurochemical which gives humans feelings of warmth toward others. Acts of compassion, sometimes termed 'the warm glow effect,' spur our bodies to create more oxytocin, which in turn encourages greater compassion.

The Dalai Lama said: 'If you want others to be happy, practise compassion.'

However, giving and other forms of compassion do more than release brain chemicals. They have been proven to reduce stress and anxiety, help with depression and indeed some studies even suggest that they improve our life span. Suffice it to say, I understand that the anterior cingulate cortex located in the brain is involved in our feelings, thinking, in memory, attention, and motivation. It has been suggested that it is active when we pray, and that it is manifest in acts of empathy, and compassion. A non-scientific rule of thumb might be brain cells work in a similar way as do our muscle cells, the more one uses brain cells the stronger they become.

Humans have a particular neuron called the Von Economo, which branches out into nearly every area of the brain. It helps us to develop social awareness skills. So, for example: the ability to read body language, to interpret a voice inflection, and to recognise facial expressions. All these processes rely on the Von Economo Neurons, relatively large cells that allow rapid communication across the relatively large brains of for example humans, great apes, elephants, and cetaceans. Practising compassion exercises and develops this important brain cell and the result is positive 'gut' feelings. I discovered that the vagus nerve aids digestion and that it is widely accepted as the 'care-taking organ' because it is engaged when we are caring for others. Research, we were informed, connects activity in the vagus nerve to feeling optimistic, improved physical health, and greater artistic appreciation.

What I discovered was that practising unconditional acts of kindness meant I feel happier, fuller, and more alive and connected to others. In transactional terms that is a 'win, win!' We can choose to leave behind the world of blame and enter a world in which compassion trumps heartlessness. I am keen to explore this topic when I return to my usual pattern of working. Will practising compassion and kindness help me become a different kind of leader, and could it enable greater capacity in others?

There are many rooms filled with love in the Father's house ... we cannot walk through all of them here but we can take tools with us for the remainder of the journey. So, turning away from Wales I move back to the North to Yorkshire and the Cumbrian lakes and mountains.

North

The Northings point true on the map,
when you walk along them, they lead to places,
somewhere along the line.

My North is peat and darkness and shafts and half-shafts of light.
North is the place of gathering where water is caught and dammed.
North is giant; it is where skies shine astral bright at night.
North is industry, moorland, and height.
The North is rock and might.
North is my hope and delight.

Adam

The first book of the Torah is Genesis. It tells us that Adam is the first human being, the first person to walk in Eden and on the earth. Adam walked in paradise before he walked in a broken and beleaguered world. Adam literally means 'from the earth.' Adam is God's gift from heaven.

Adam and his family are members of one of my church congregations. Adam has some interesting views on faith and morality. He is a staunch supporter of those who adopt a faith position, and he has become a valued friend and teacher. During the

Covid lockdown he reintroduced me to a beautiful part of my local countryside pictured on the front of this book, Ramsden Clough. I think had he not encouraged me to walk in this valley retreat I may have faded in those days of isolation and home working.

Adam is not from Yorkshire, that does not count in any way against him. He is from Kent. So, Adam shared with me that many of his holidays as a youngster were taken in the Lake District following rail travel from their family home. Adam as a youngster was able to share in his parents' passion and he began exploring the fells and mountainsides and grew in appreciation for maps, topography, walking and running.

Adam introduced me to his passion and the days I have spent walking with him since across the northern parts of the Black Peak, on our home territory, or in the Lakes have been moments of glory. Adam makes navigation easy. He moves swiftly and joyfully across the land and makes informative, knowledgeable observations as he moves. He is easy to be with and his wisdom is vast. Everything appears more possible with him, he has a great sense of humour mixed with optimism and he exemplifies compassion for others.

We shared a day walking in the Central Fells. Parking at the National Trust car park in Great Langdale at the head of the valley setting off in damp drizzle up what is known as The Band, then taking the lower route on to the Great Slab. This striking geographical feature looked as if it had been lifted out of the ground only the day before we arrived. We then moved up onto one of Wainwright's favourite fells, Bowfell at 2,959 feet high. The rain was abating but the visibility was still limited with occasional hopeful glints of blue sky appearing as gaps in the silver light which covered the fell tops. We then descended to Ore Gap before climbing Esk Pike then crossing Esk Hause and up onto the summit of Great End. This was a treat to behold with views now appearing back across the Slab and up and beyond to the Scafell group, and behind us the Langdales dappled by the sun, rising in all their glory.

Walking down the Fell side I took a photograph of the stone cross seat constructed for hikers to rest upon and eat their snacks before ascending to the top of Allen Crags. There we could see Ingleborough some forty-plus miles away to the south in the Yorkshire Dales National Park. Northwards we could make out the borders of Scotland. Crossing Tongue Head we descended past Angle Tarn, again gaining height onto Rosset Pike. Here we paused to take pictures across the valley towards the Langdale Pikes now in full sunshine and majestically clothed in graphite grey, purple, green and blue. The Pikes appeared beset with jewels set in a crown. We then skirted a less obvious path below the craggy outcrop down to Stake Gill, picking up the Cumbria Way back down to the car park: 4,152 feet of up and down, 11 miles of footpaths and fell, over six and half hours of joyous walking. I honestly felt that I was walking in paradise, and I captured for a moment a restored vision of the world.

I have seldom felt this degree of happiness. Adam may have been put outside the gates of Eden but we are potentially able look upon its aura and remember. The ultimate place of arrival to which I believe we are moving retains the capacity to inspire us in the present.

**Figure 27. The stone cross below Great End – a good place to enjoy a snack
This is one of the central crossings for hikers in the Lakes**

Reflecting philosophically and theologically on the essence of who I am, or how I am as I enter the next phase of ministry has been valuable for me. Throughout these months a process of review and improvement of character and lifestyle has taken place. It began with recognition of failure and three months walking has returned me to an improved sense of being and wholeness. To revisit the gardening metaphor, the clearing I made early on is now a fertile space, new shoots of life are growing and in some places I feel I am able to harvest good fruit. I am happier, less stressed, surer footed, accepting of the realities and imperfections that surround me. Perhaps like the snow, when I am gone I will be entirely what I was made to be beyond physical being.

One's physical being has substance, but we are each greater than the sum of our outputs. There is a short passage in Matthew's Gospel at Chapter 10:39 (NIV); it speaks powerfully to me now, *'Whoever finds their life will lose it, and whoever loses their life for my sake will find it.'*

In a single instant on the 22nd of May 2022, on the mountainside I felt as I have never felt before: lost, abandoned and deeply unhappy. My plan was shot through and full of holes only four hours into the walking. I was deeply disappointed with myself, my lack of self-perception and arrogance. I could have determinedly gone on and physically I would have prevailed but would I have engaged in a process of self-discovery and have been able to stop and 'smell the roses'? I have concluded that enjoyment does indeed matter and that there is a definite place for happiness. *'What do workers gain from their toil? I know that there is nothing better for people than to be happy and to do good while they live. That each of them may eat and drink and find satisfaction in all their toil this is the gift of God.'* [Ecclesiastes 3:9,12-13 NIV] My son's text message and wisdom saved me from myself; he introduced a new variable into the process of sabbatical, my enjoyment.

Throughout the whole of my life, for as long as I can remember I have always felt I have had to be able to depend upon myself and not be dependent on others.

In some contexts that is good news because I believe in other people's abilities to do more than they often believe they are capable of. It strengthens a ministry of encouragement.

However, for me it was all coming to a head before I had taken a single step. I was exhausted and wearied by the vagaries of a busy working life. I needed to give myself permission to take a break, something I did not find it easy to admit to myself. I needed to confess that if I was ever going to heal my mind, soul, and body I had to give myself over to the divine worker and look squarely at what the creation has been pointing me towards. The following months of walking led me to a new place in my life where I have a newfound relaxed confidence. I think that I have developed a new compassionate resilience, a continuing love for the environment and deeper respect for the people who came and walked with me, and perhaps for those who have walked with me previously. Those who know me, and who took time to care for me. They have helped me to be happy and have renewed in me the value of friendship and companionship, something I had lost touch with.

As time went on, I was able to plan walks more confidently. I invested in some new equipment and took pleasure in it. Physically I became more accustomed to Lakeland fell walking. My diet changed for the better. Friends and family came to join me. The Cumbrian rain eventually abated. The sun came out, not only literally but figuratively. I gradually began to turn a corner. I had been holding on too tightly to my fears, managing decline, working with impossible odds and unrealistic expectations, and living carefully even fearfully at every turn. I had almost lost the ability to think positively about anything. Slowly I let go and started to breathe. Today I feel more optimistic and positive about the now. The future is something that the evangelist Matthew reflects upon.

'Therefore I tell you, do not worry about your life, what you will eat or drink; or about your body, what you will wear. Is not life more than food, and the body more than clothes? Look at the birds of the air; they do not sow or reap or store away in barns, and yet your heavenly Father feeds them. Are you not much more valuable than they? Can any one of you by worrying add a single hour to your life? But seek first his kingdom and his righteousness, and all these things will be given to you as well. Therefore do not worry about tomorrow, for tomorrow will worry about itself. Each day has enough trouble of its own.' [Matthew 6: 25 -27 & 33-34 NIV].

I was signed to an internet article about C S Lewis who said that 'The Christian life is simply a process of having your natural self 'changed' into a Christ self.' What Lewis meant by this was, to find yourself you must lose yourself entirely in Christ. Lewis' definition reiterates the words attributed to St Paul from Ephesians, *'You were taught, with regard to your former way of life, to put off your old self, which is being corrupted; ... and to put on the new self, created to be like God in true righteousness and holiness.'* [Ephesians 4:22-24 NIV].

Lewis explained that the change from the old to the new self occurs very deep inside the person. That such a change takes time and that through such transformation one becomes the person who one is truly meant to be. I am reminded of a time in the 1990s standing in the big top at the Greenbelt Festival with my friend Angus watching Bruce Cockburn perform 'Soul of a Man' a gospel blues song first recorded by Blind Willie Johnson in 1930.

'Well won't somebody tell me. Answer if you can!
I want somebody to tell me. Just what is the soul of a man?'

Whilst all this walking might appear to be something of a selfish pursuit, I am guessing God's desire is to work with us in person, not always through a congregation or even a bishop's chrism.

My soul or eternal salvation I believe is safe, but surely there is more to learn about life and living. Beyond my physical existence I am also the epicentre of my experiences.

I am self-aware, conscious. Being able to reflect during this sabbatical period has led to greater self-awareness not only of what needed cultivating and caring for but of greater opportunity and capacity for goodness. Each one of us recognises ourselves as distinct from the rest of the cosmos as we move through it. It is 'I' who experience these thoughts, feelings, reactions, and the 'I' is shaped by them, just as time and the weather shapes the landscape. When talking with those who have crossed the fells with me what has been revealed is a rich interior life that is uniquely our own, one which needs just as much care and attention as the exterior public life.

So, Ivy, how can I give an account of being an object in the world alongside my inner life and my personal experiences? As both an object and a subject am I able to piece together a full picture of what and who I am. Whether walking into or away from: I am I, and I am no other. There is only one me and he is not invincible. Like every other human being he is fragile and full of vulnerabilities. Recognizing this while the *'Slings and arrows of outrageous fortune'* [Hamlet Act III scene i] fall around one compels me sometimes to walk away from rather than into all that is life giving.

I am following a Netflix series called *Sandman*. The gist of the story goes: The Sandman is a cosmic being who controls all dreams; he is captured and held prisoner for more than a century; upon securing freedom he must journey across different worlds and timelines to fix the chaos his absence has caused.

Some of the time on the high mountain passes, walking through cloud and fog I have lost awareness of time and space. I learnt to simply follow the arrow on the compass and trust that the laws of nature would deliver me from the chaos and restore me to the light. It has felt at times like I have been crossing timelines. The ones which run through my life, the intersection of education, family, friendships, relationships work and ministry. And, of course, being a husband and a father. My friend is whispering in my ear again: 'There is no going back.' But there is a sense in which one can go on and adapt, and live differently with new priorities.

Richard Rohr, in <u>*Falling Upward: A Spirituality for the Two Halves of Life*</u> (San Francisco: Jossey-Bass, 2011, 153–154, 160) writes: '*We tend to think of the second part of our lives as getting old, dealing with health issues, and letting go of our physical life.*' He continues, '*That which looks like falling, can largely be experienced as falling upward and onward into a broader deeper world where the soul has found its fullness, and is finally connected to the whole, and lives inside the Big Picture.*'

Is that what I have been doing as I have gone up these mountains? Have I been falling upwards, not just literally but spiritually reaching out into the cosmos, looking for meaning and purpose within my field of vision? Have the views from the top offered a new perspective on the demands, importance, and joys of serving others as a priest in the Church? I think so. Crossing Lingmoor Fell on the 18th of July was joyous. The sun was high in the sky when I set off from the National Trust Car Park at Elterwater. As I ascended the 1,538 feet I was filled with a sense of contentment and happiness. Everything I saw appeared to shine. Was I finally happy? Stopping work to rest and reflect has encouraged me to count my blessings, and to cleave to that which is important and good.

As I descended Helm Crag just above Grassmere with Simon, having completed the well-trodden Green Burn Round on Saturday 13th August and 101 of the 214 Wainwright peaks, I knew I was coming to the end of this part of the journey.

The world I had largely left behind was coming back into view. I was still walking in these mountains, yet the bigger picture was looming. Will there be things that need fixing when I get back to work? Is there any willingness on my part to reconnect to people and their stories and traditions that in the scheme of things have not always been good for me? Does God want me to be happy and is happiness only available through work? I felt the creep in my sleep. I began to feel restless for knowledge about the people and the church. I estimate that I have walked, across 224 miles and climbed 68,153 feet of the Lake District (twice the height of Everest).

Fig 28. Sean and Simon walking the Greenburn Round on my last day of sabbatical

Discovery

What do I think I have uncovered or discovered?

Walking in solitude is not a pastime for the lonely and broken.
Healing is in friendship and union, in community and it is peaceable.
People matter more than things, but things have their place;
they make our lives easier.
We are not the sum of our achievements rather they reflect our ambition.
Walking is a great leveler: status is not attached to it.
Mountains, Fells and Tarns are paradoxically beautiful and dangerous.
The weather conditions change everything.
Knowledge of your environment is essential.
A warm sleeping bag makes for pleasant dreams.
Feet connect us to the earth;
we are made from the same cosmic dust as the earth.
Love, care, respect, and honour matter.
Never be afraid to admit failure.
Tend to your bruises early.
Come again with a different plan on another day.
Enjoy the moment!
Believe in yourself and trust others.
Black toes will turn pink again.

Reflecting on the sabbatical period I discovered that it might be possible to live more compassionately, with less angst and to be unafraid of the demons that play to our trauma and anxieties.

Walking into myself walked me into a deeper love, love for those who care for me and ultimately into the love of God in whose image we are each made. That image can become distorted in anyone, and for those who are on their frontlines most days that distortion or disturbance can accumulate more than it ought. In the future I aim to live with less fear, to face conflict squarely, and to be kinder to myself and others. Of course, we can ask questions concerning our care for God's world, and God's people. But I would prefer we should not do that in isolation, without considering what would help each of us as individuals to thrive and grow. There is a great tradition of sacrifice involved in faith communities: maybe we should not be so quick to lay down our own lives. Behind these reflections lurk others: the shape I am being cast in by established religion, the effort it takes to resist. The often-seeming self-centered politics of the age. The threat of waging of wars.

Speaking of this world Hamlet says, '*Fie on't! Oh fie! 'tis an unweeded garden, / That grows to seed; things rank and gross in nature / Possess it merely.*' [Hamlet Act I scene ii] The weeding out of mine appears to have been worthwhile. The pressures have lessened; they remain but somehow being on sabbatical and walking has given me some distance from them. They appear less powerful and threatening. The pruned me looks more agile of mind, body, and my soul appears to feel lighter. I might hope that there are new things growing in my life that might bear fruit for others: writing this reflection might be a signpost to a different centre of being for me and indeed for anyone who reads it.

The journey I have made has been with people who have my best interests at their heart and for that, I am most thankful. However, I wonder if they and others will be able to accommodate this different version of me, or if once back in the breach I will return to type. Will the insight I have gained, the disciplines I have practised, the new techniques I have learned desert me or I them? Will recuperation and rest fade like an old photograph left on the mantelpiece in its frame in the sun? It was right for this season but now back to the real world not a magical one with a Sandman fixing the universe, rather one in which chaos and anarchy often appear to have the final say, and where most folks these days appear to want the way of the law rather than the way of love. Some degree of cynicism about the future still lurks behind what has been a rich time for me, my family, and friends.

I have missed the regularity of the Church liturgy, the music and sharing of the sacrament with my congregations, all important defining moments that are so much a part of my life. On the walk I stopped and prayed in many small churches on valley sides and bottoms. I rather think that the Underskiddaw Church Room in Applethwaite, and the church in Martindale dedicated to Martin of Tours rank amongst my favourites. How these buildings remain open is as much of a mystery sometimes as the faith that is practised in them. So, few people appear to be involved in them, yet they remain essential in some way to the life of the community which surrounds them. Years ago, on placement whilst training for ministry I was travelling with David Fowler. He was then Rector of Kirkoswald, Renwick and Ainstable in the Penrith Deanery. We sped many miles out into the sticks to his church congregation. We arrived to lead Evensong and waiting were six or so people, all elderly. They faithfully prayed the liturgy, sang the psalms and hymns, made the coffee and shared their home baked cake. On the journey home David must have been able to read my mind. He said to me, 'Sean, that's not the failed congregation of the church. It is the congregation.' I have never forgotten that most salient observation.

My spiritual director often quotes from Nehemiah 8:10 '*The joy of the Lord is your strength.*' I'm looking forward to worship and prayer with other Christians in the Holme Valley Churches.

Not having Scout my dog with me was a dampener at times, especially when not overly warm in a sleeping bag in the early mornings. He was not there to lie with me, and I felt that each time I left him I was betraying the bond we share. On the other hand, my wife was delighted to have him home with her. I, however, believe that those early days would have been easier if Scout had been with me. On the fells I would have felt less afraid walking into darkness. Knowing Scout was just ahead of me checking the trail as he has always done would have been an indicator of safety. On the days we did walk together we savoured the moments, and I gladly shared my sandwich crusts, it felt like a moment of communion although I recognize it was not...

Orrest Head overlooks Windermere. The walk starts on the A591 by the large 'Orrest Head' sign and follows a lane which wends its way through woodland for most of the 20-minute journey to the top. It is a short circular walk and importantly was Alfred Wainwright's first window into the Lake District. He described it as being, '*Where we came in, our first ascent in Lakeland, our first sight of mountains in tumultuous array across glittering waters, our awakening to beauty.*' It remains a popular walk and one that I now take each time I depart the Lakeland. Looking out one cannot fail but to give thanks. It was my finishing point. Walking the fells had made me happy and I wanted to look out on them and be with them as one might an old friend. Wainwright again commenting eschatologically and more profoundly than I am able, '*Dare we hope there will be another Orrest Head over the threshold of the next heaven?*' Like Alfred Wainwright I too hope so.

So, Sean, did you complete your walk or was it a pilgrimage? I did and there are still more fells and vales to cross, dwell in and discover. I did not do everything I had planned, but I did do what was necessary and fruitful. And I know the route back to a place and people I have become even closer to. I know why hikers climb these peaks time and time again and I want to climb some of them again. Going up presents not only a physical challenge but on clear days the views are breathtaking. Awe and wonder bring with them a sense of well-being and contentment. Every day on the fell produces a different challenge. I aim to continue to keep walking.

It took me three attempts to complete my first Lakeland walk. I climbed up the 2,863 feet of Fairfield three times during the three months I was walking in the Lakes. Not once was the weather kind, and twice it was brutal. I finally completed my first walk from the top of Fairfield concluding with Hart Crag, Dove Crag, High Pike and Low Pike on the 25th of July. After crossing Low Sweden Bridge I walked in the late, hot afternoon sun and rain, following the Rainbow along the short road into Ambleside where I went into Apple Pie a well know local café and ordered a double shot latte and a vanilla slice. I think Charlie Mackesy who wrote and illustrated *The Boy, the Mole, the Fox and the Horse* maybe got the answer without needing to cross one fell or climb a single mountain:

'Do you have a favourite saying?' asked the boy.
'Yes,' said the Mole.
'What is it?'
'If at first you don't succeed have some cake.'
'I see, does it work?'
'Every time.'

Figure 29. Latte and Cake at Apple Pie Ambleside, Cumbria

Afterthought

Cornwall Sept 2022

Cornwall is the place where we have enjoyed family holidays for the last 17 years. Whilst on holiday in Cornwall this year, walking across the top of Treyarnon Bay, my wife Sally pulled me close to her and spoke with her loving wisdom into my heart. 'This is a time of change for us,' she whispered dreamily. 'Our children are growing up, our lives are changing.' Usually, such sentiment would inspire in me anxiety and blind panic but this time I felt excited about us and about the future. There was nothing else to say. We held each other in our arms and watched the morning sun make its westward journey over the blue sea, into the sky, up to the heavenlies to re-establish the new day. For me on the journey from mountain to seashore sometimes it felt like our very lives were being negotiated. Those feelings of thankfulness, deep affection, respect, and love for my wife all washed over me like the waves on this beach. Washing over the shores of my being. I had arrived home. I was in the arms of the one person in this world who chose me before all others and has always had in her heart my well-being and best interests. Finally, I can stop running. I am no longer afraid.

Then, in the afternoon, news came that Queen Elizabeth II had died at Balmoral in Scotland. It all came rushing back to me in this moment, change had been flowing this way for some time. Change came when my mother-in-law died during the Covid pandemic, and change came before that too when God called us to be with one another and to ministry in the Church. Suddenly I felt a long way from our Church fellowship. Like us, they were reeling at the news of Her Majesty's passing. The passing of a life, of an institutional figurehead, of a servant, of a constant heartbeat that stood for stability and modesty, yet one that was courageous, progressive and willing to embrace change whilst being faithful and hopeful about the future.

'Life in its fullness' John 10:10 is not something to be collated at the end of one's life; it is not the sum of many things. It is not the eulogy. Life is one continuous thing until it ends. Then maybe we are reborn in some other sphere of being and belonging. Life is this day and age. It is visceral and immediate. Life is not to be feared. Waiting for it to happen will not stop its timeless march onward to a time when we are not, when I am not. Then it will be the time for the eulogy.

'Sean, walk into yourself ...' Ivy, my dear friend, I have found by walking that without the others there is no meaning or purpose to anything. We cannot live abundantly in isolation or fear. We are informed by St Paul that this life is merely a pale reflection, a mirror image of what one day will be. Ivy, I have been walking into a new love for life, for God's people, for my family. Have I enjoyed some semblance of well-being, and healing? I feel more alive. Am I living now with an improved perspective and a new curiosity? I believe I am and better equipped to face the new and future challenges in ministry because I am more accepting of the present realities.

Today those 'slings and arrows' [Hamlet Act III scene i] appear to have a weakened power over me. Nature, time, and walking have drawn the toxins from me, perhaps partly on to these pages. Maybe writing is the therapy – *therapeia*, Greek: 'to minister to' – simply to reflect and to record the passion and blessing. The original Greek meaning reminds one that our calling is to minister the Good News. Having walked into myself, I confidently step forward to resume the greater pilgrimage I am compelled to complete that is my life.

"And then my heart with pleasure fills,

Figure 30. Sally, William and Lydia and me…our family

And dances with the daffodils."

William Wordsworth

My thanks to:

Leeds Diocese, EIG, Boniface Trust, Fellowship of St John for their kind sponsorship.

The Taigh Mor Foundation.

My family: Sally, William and Lydia and my niece Anna Jackman-Smith who is a Wainwright veteran.

My friend Professor Ivy George, for encouraging me to ask myself the right questions.

Rev Mike Newman CF. VR & VW transporter owner and colleague.

Woody and Dave, friends who showed walking determination and delivered in both the field and the bar unequalled hospitality.

Professors Adam Nelson and Simon Barrans for their friendship and knowledge, and for knowing which questions not to ask me.

Rev Dr Stephen Dixon and Rev Ailsa Brooke trusted colleagues who gave their time so I could have this time.

Clinton and Jean for the extended use of their Lake District hideaway.

Alex Hobson and Alastair Ross who read my early manuscripts and made helpful and insightful comments.

Rev Dr Stephen Dixon for being a longtime trusted friend and colleague, and for supporting the editing of this script with questions, concerns and stamina.

Rev John Hayward, for his support and interest during editing.

All pitfalls, mistakes and typos are entirely my own.

And lastly to my team parish, especially Christ Church and St Thomas' congregants for sharing this life, and gifting me this time.

All Scripture quotations, unless otherwise indicated, are taken from the Holy Bible, New International Version®, NIV®. Copyright ©1973, 1978, 1984, 2011 by Biblica, Inc.™ Used by permission of Zondervan. All rights reserved worldwide.www.zondervan.com

The "NIV" and "New International Version" are trademarks registered in the United States Patent and Trademark Office by Biblica, Inc.™

Under Skiddaw